The STRAIT PATH TO REAL ESTATE WEALTH

KRIS KROHN

REIC PRESS

The information in this book is not presented as a source of tax, financial, investment, or legal advice. The information and any data contained herein have been obtained from sources which are believed to be reliable, but the author and publisher do not represent that they are accurate or complete, and the information and data should not be relied upon as such. All opinions expressed and data provided herein are subject to change without notice. Past performance is no guarantee of future results, and current performance may be lower or higher than the information presented. Results shown in these materials are not typical, results will vary. The author and publisher do not assume any responsibility for actions or non-actions taken by people who have read this book, and no one shall be entitled to a claim for detrimental reliance or otherwise based upon any information provided or expressed herein. Your use of any information provided here does not constitute any type of contractual relationship between yourself and the provider(s) of this information. Neither the author nor the publisher is providing any investment advice or recommendations. Individuals should always conduct their own research and due diligence and obtain tax, financial, investment and legal professional advice before making any investment decision. The information contained here is general in nature and is not intended as tax, financial, investment, or legal advice. The information contained herein may not be applicable to or suitable for the individuals' specific circumstances or needs and may require consideration of other matters.

Published by REIC Press
1070 E 800 N
Orem, UT 84097

Copyright ©2010 Kris Krohn

All rights reserved under all copyright conventions.

No part of this book may be reproduced, stored in a retrieval system, or transmitted by any means, electronic, mechanical, photocopying, recording, or otherwise, without written permission from the publisher.

Design and composition by Greenleaf Book Group LLC
Cover design by Greenleaf Book Group LLC

The terms Strait Path, Strait Path Real Estate, and Compassionate Financing are trademarks registered with the United States Patent and Trademark Office and are owned by the author.

Cataloging-in-Publication data
(Prepared by The Donohue Group, Inc.)

Krohn, Kris.
 The Strait path to real estate wealth / Kris Krohn. -- 1st ed.

 p. : ill. ; cm.

 Includes bibliographical references.
 ISBN: 978-0-9843026-1-1

1. Strait Path System. 2. Real estate investment. 3. Finance, Personal. 4. House buying. I. REIC. II. Title.

HD1382.5 .K76 2010
332.6324   2010922614

Part of the Tree Neutral™ program, which offsets the number of trees consumed in the production and printing of this book by taking proactive steps, such as planting trees in direct proportion to the number of trees used: www.treeneutral.com

Printed in the United States of America on acid-free paper

11 12 13 14 15 16   10 9 8 7 6 5 4 3 2 1

First Edition

CONTENTS

INTRODUCTION 1
The Best Form of Real Estate • Don't Just Learn Real Estate—Do It • Why Most Real Estate Investors Fail • Why the Name "Strait Path Real Estate"? • Six Core Elements of Investing: Time, Effort, Risk, Service, Market Conditions, Profit • Hybrid Methodology • How the System Was Created • System Proven Through More than 700 Real Transactions

1—THE CRUCIAL MENTAL SHIFT: OVERCOMING AMERICA'S BROKEN FINANCIAL PARADIGM 13
Don't Get on the Strait Path Until You Have the Right Mind-Set • The Accumulation Mind-Set & the 401(k) Trap • The Home Equity Pitfall • What Is an Investor? • How to Develop the Investor Mind-Set • Do What Actually Works, Not What You *Think* Should Work

2—OVERVIEW OF THE STRAIT PATH SYSTEM 33
Understand Big-Picture Context Before Details • Four Core Phases: Plan, Find, Purchase, Serve • Portfolio Game Plan • How to Find Extremely Discounted Real Estate • How to Purchase the Most Properties • Compassionate Financing • Achieving Critical Mass

3—THE SIX ELEMENTS OF SUCCESSFUL INVESTING: VARIOUS METHODS COMPARED AND CONTRASTED 49
A Holistic Approach to Real Estate Wealth • How Much Time, Effort & Risk Does Your Investment Strategy Take? • Does Your Strategy Serve or Exploit Individuals & Society? • Will Your Strategy Work in Every Market, or Just Booming Markets? • Five Profit Centers: Discount Equity, Cash Flow, Down Payment, Appreciation, Tax Benefits • Strait Path Compared & Contrasted with Rentals, Flips & Lease Options

4—CREATING YOUR PORTFOLIO GAME PLAN 77
Begin with the End in Mind • Identify & Leverage Hidden Assets • Financial Assets & Relationships • Create Your 10-Year Game Plan • Four Approaches to the Strait Path • Achieve Critical Mass Through Endurance

5—FINDING INVESTMENT PROPERTIES 95
You Make Money When You Buy, Not When You Sell • Three Criteria for Finding the Best Properties • Only Purchase Below the Median Home Price • Purchase in Livable Condition • Buy Only with 15% Equity or More • How to Leverage the MLS & Realtors Effectively • How to Evaluate Potential Investments & Perform a Comprehensive Market Analysis • Negotiations the Strait Path Way

6—PURCHASING INVESTMENT PROPERTIES 129

How to Qualify for Loans • Understand Your Purchase Appraisal • Profit-Conscious vs. Rate Conscious • How to Finance Multiple Properties & Protect Your Future Portfolio • How to Optimize Your Debt-to-Income Ratio • Protect Yourself from "Lemon" Properties

7—COMPASSIONATE FINANCING: PROFIT THROUGH SERVICE 147

Compassionate Financing: The Benefits of Lease Options, But Without the Flaws • Why You Should Give Tenants More Control—& Responsibility • Elements of a Lease Option Contract • How Compassionate Financing Is Different—& Better—than Lease Options • How to Market & Execute Compassionate Financing Contracts

8—ACHIEVING CRITICAL MASS 171

Achieve Critical Mass Through Discipline • The Importance & Power of Delaying Gratification • How to Achieve Exponential Growth on the Strait Path • How to Enjoy Infinite Returns • The Power of Collaboration • Build Your Power Team

9—FINANCIAL LIBERATION: MOVING FROM MECHANICS TO MEANING 187

Why This Book Isn't About Real Estate • Financial Liberation Has Nothing to do with Money • Myths & Fallacies that Limit Financial Liberation • Find & Live Meaning Through Wise Stewardship

CONCLUSION–FROM "WHAT IF?" TO "WHAT NEXT?" 203

Avoid Regret by Acting • The Tragedy of Lost Opportunity Costs • Are You Open to Possibility?

ACKNOWLEDGMENTS 207

APPENDIX A–HOW TO JOIN REAL ESTATE INVESTMENT COMPANIES AND GET ON THE STRAIT PATH 211

APPENDIX B—FREE DOWNLOADS AND RESOURCES 213

APPENDIX C—RECOMMENDED READING 215

INDEX 217

Dedication

This book is dedicated to all our Strait Path investors. Without your confidence, trust, and willingness to take the "road less traveled," Real Estate Investment Companies never would have succeeded.

Introduction

You have probably already seen dozens of books about how to get rich in real estate, so I'm going to slash through the clutter with a bold claim: *The real estate system you'll learn in this book takes the least time, effort, and risk, creates the most value for society, and generates the greatest returns for more investors in any given market than any other system you will ever encounter*. I'm confident that this system is the *best* form of real estate investing. That's both a promise and a challenge. I challenge any reader to find any other system or strategy that is on par with this one in a comprehensive comparison.

I don't mean to be arrogant; I simply value your time. You have important things to do with your life, and reading this book is an investment in time and effort. I recognize and appreciate that. I want to make your experience as worthwhile as possible. Ultimately, I want your investment to pay actual dividends as you become a profitable real estate investor. In fact, that's one of the core differences you'll come to appreciate between this system and others. I don't make money by selling knowledge—I make money by helping people apply knowledge to succeed in real estate.

To date, Real Estate Investment Companies (REIC), which I created to leverage my proprietary Strait Path investment system, has helped hundreds of clients invest profitably in real estate. Not a single person has ever lost money long-term using our system. Our average investor enjoys a more than 50 percent annual return on investment, purchases investment properties that contain at least 15 percent equity, and often increases his or her net worth by $50,000 with each investment purchase. Our company continues to multiply its productivity and profits in some of the worst years for real estate. We're not in the business of teaching real estate—we're in the business of *doing* real estate.

If real estate investing can be this profitable, then why do so few investors succeed? First of all, it's because real estate investing is *hard*. There's no way around that fact. No matter how good the system, real estate is a tremendous challenge for most people. It requires tons of specialized knowledge, a productive mind-set, persistence, working with frustrating situations and annoying people, and continuous problem solving. However, having the right knowledge, system, and support can make all the difference.

Most investors, unaware that there is another option, are faced with two choices. Choice one is to attempt to invest on their own, with little knowledge and experience. Such investors almost always choose systems and strategies that require too much time, effort, money, and risk. Perhaps they get burned out with rentals or flips. They dabble in short sales and foreclosures until they realize how hard it is to manage these investments. They may over-leverage and lose everything. When they fail, they become disillusioned and give up on real estate altogether.

The second choice is to pay between $5,000 and $50,000 to "gurus" who make more money selling information than from actual real estate investing. They offer no support, no hands-on training, and no real implementation. The money students of these gurus pay usually goes toward a generic educational system. This means that 1) the system doesn't get applied, and 2) the system doesn't teach students the *best* form of real estate investing. These guru systems may get student investors motivated for a time, but they're incomplete and leave students hanging without ever buying a property. As a result, for most investors this is money down the drain.

Ironically, most people first get excited about real estate investing by seeing others succeed, and by reading books and attending seminars. They become convinced that real estate will help them become wealthier quicker, with less effort, money, knowledge, and risk than other paths. Indeed it *can*, but you must apply the right system.

Real Estate Investment Companies (REIC) Investors Share Their Experience: Chris and Sheralyn

"We decided that we wanted to start investing in real estate about a year ago. After trying a few network marketing companies, we realized that that wasn't going to be our path to wealth. We didn't know how to do real estate—we just knew there was money to be made. We started by purchasing books and materials and researching various systems and educational programs.

"Wanting a more hands-on approach, we signed up for a $2,000 program. After we mastered that introductory package, they upsold us to their $20,000 package, which we paid willingly, thinking that it would give us the tools and resources we needed to succeed. They were supposed to show us exactly how to do each step and help us along the way, but it never happened like they promised. In fact, they don't even return our calls anymore.

"After this disappointment, we met Kris Krohn, who introduced us to his Strait Path system. We started warming up as Kris and his associates counseled us on a few decisions. We had been looking at a duplex with the goal of living in one side and renting out the other. It sounded like a good idea to us, but Kris's team pointed out a number of flaws that we were unaware of, one of them being that we were paying more than market value for the property. They pointed out all the reasons it was a risky deal, and that's when we realized that Kris and the Strait Path system were the real deal—REIC actually *invested* in real estate instead of just *teaching* about it.

"Soon after joining REIC we purchased our first investment, which at a 15 percent equity position immediately increased our net worth by $37,000. Since we were renting at the time, we moved into this first home. Our plan is to refinance it soon to purchase our next investment. In addition, our home has an apartment that we're fixing up to meet legal requirements, and we'll rent it out to help offset our mortgage.

"The Strait Path is a slower game plan than a lot of the hyped systems we've seen, and we've really learned to appreciate that because there's a much smaller margin of error and much lower risk. What sets it apart from the other systems we've researched and worked with is that it's actually based on implementation."

What if all of the reasons for real estate–investing failure could be eliminated? What if there were a program that provided both education and hands-on implementation? What if there were a coherent, comprehensive, and predictable system that *anyone* could apply to succeed in real estate without any of the risk and hassle that has dragged down investors in the past? What if there were *one* real estate investment system that was better than any other? How could it change your life? I feel blessed to have discovered such a system, which I call Strait Path real estate.

The name of the system comes from a verse in the King James Bible. Matthew 7:13–14 says, "Enter ye in at the strait gate: for wide is the gate, and broad is the way, that leadeth to destruction, and many there be which go in thereat: Because strait is the gate, and narrow is the way, which leadeth unto life, and few there be that find it." I'll leave the pursuit of eternal life up to you. My purpose is to apply the metaphor to real estate and prove that there is *one* sure way to real estate wealth for the vast majority of investors—though few people ever find it. Everything else is a "broad and crooked" path that leads to "destruction," or in other words, investment failure.

The passage continues in verses 15–20: "Beware of false prophets, which come to you in sheep's clothing, but inwardly they are ravening wolves. Ye shall know them by their fruits. Do men gather grapes of thorns, or figs of thistles? Even so every good tree bringeth forth good fruit; but a corrupt tree bringeth forth evil fruit. A good tree cannot bring forth evil fruit, neither can a corrupt tree bring forth good fruit. Every tree that bringeth not forth good fruit is hewn down, and cast into the fire. Wherefore by their fruits ye shall know them."

Remove the religious context from these verses and just consider the imagery. It's highly applicable because there are so many competing theories of real estate investing. Some "gurus" make far more money selling knowledge than they do investing in real estate. Their teachings can be benign yet ineffective, or even harmful and misleading. Many forms of real estate investing result in little more than stress, heartache, and financial loss. Discernment comes when we examine the "fruits" of all teachings and strategies. I've already spoken of the fruits of Strait Path real estate. My purpose in writing this book is to invite you to step onto that undeviating path so that you, too, can enjoy those fruits.

The biblical metaphor will help you fully grasp the power of the real estate system you're in the process of learning. If the claim I made in the first paragraph of this introduction is true, then you can reject the flaws of all other real estate investment systems and strategies and leverage a perfected, foolproof system. You can slice through complexity and risk and skip right to the core of safe, sustainable profits. You can abandon past failures and financial detours, embrace hope, and take diligent action. You can retire far sooner than you thought possible and fund your dreams by building a healthy real estate portfolio.

SIX CORE ELEMENTS OF INVESTING: IN SEARCH OF THE *BEST* FORM OF REAL ESTATE

All these successes are possible *if* you stay on the right path. The path is so strait and narrow and carries such strict guidelines because there are many critical aspects of investing to account for. Specifically, there are six core elements to consider when comparing investment strategies: 1) time, 2) effort, 3) risk, 4) service (Does it create sustainable value for people?), 5) market conditions (Will it work in any market?), and 6) profit. Each of these elements is critical to successful investing. More important, however, is the fact that your decisions and strategies must account for all of them collectively.

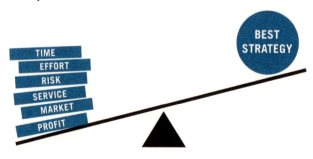

If you take me up on my challenge to find a better real estate system than the Strait Path system, understand that your comparisons must take all six of these elements into consideration. The system must be superior on the whole, rather than just in one particular area. In my experience, few systems consider more than three elements, and almost none consider all six. This is one of the primary factors that makes Strait Path real estate so powerful.

HYBRID METHODOLOGY

A key factor contributing to the effectiveness of the Strait Path system is the hybrid methodology I used in its development. I voraciously studied every form of real estate available to most investors, including rentals, fix-and-flips, foreclosures, lease options, spec building, land development, multi-unit, and commercial, among others. I identified the strengths and weaknesses of each. Then, I researched and analyzed how to incorporate the strengths of each while eliminating their weaknesses. The result was the Strait Path system. To give just a few examples, the Strait Path system incorporates the cash flow aspect of rentals but eliminates the stress and hassle of property management. It helps investors buy properties with foreclosure discounts, but without foreclosure complexity. It assimilates the strengths of lease options but rejects the exploitation commonly present in lease optioning. This hybrid approach is explored in greater detail throughout the book.

THE FOUNDATIONS OF THE STRAIT PATH SYSTEM

Of course, I didn't start my real estate–investing career with the clarity I now have. In 2002 I was attending college to become a doctor. Like most people, I wanted a high-paying, honorable career that would bring me financial security and fulfillment. I was entrenched in the "get good grades, go to college, get job security" mind-set. While in college, a few things happened that altered my perceptions and set me on a new path.

Pushing gurneys in the emergency room for an internship was exciting, but after a year of painful science and math courses, the realization of the monumental task ahead of me sank in. I would be in school for another thirteen years—and I didn't even enjoy my current classes.

Since I started college with almost no money and I wanted to avoid debt as much as possible, I got a job doing telemarketing. In my first year of phone sales, I spoke with more than 1,000 people, all of whom were asking me how to become financially successful. Most of them were over forty years old, had attended college, and had good jobs. They also had a lot of debt, and through my conversations with them, I sensed their fear and desperation. I realized that I was headed along the same path they had taken. I wondered whether I was destined for the same fate, and their desperation began to transfer to me.

During this time, I stumbled across a quote from the Social Security Board that uprooted my financial paradigm. "At age sixty-five," the quote read, "75 percent of all Americans are dependent on relatives, family, and charity; 23 percent are still working; and only 2 percent are financially independent." I was stunned. I would be in school for over a decade, spend years paying off school loans—all in a career that wasn't fulfilling to me—and I would still have a 98 percent chance of financial failure?! I was determined to discover what the successful 2 percent were doing.

I realized that the most financially successful individuals had created forms of residual income, meaning they got paid whether they were physically working or not. The rest of us had to *keep working* to earn an income. I vowed to get out of the rut and began a quest to find *my* form of residual income.

That year I married my beautiful wife, Kalenn. But with the many responsibilities of a newlywed, my desperation hit an all-time high. I was working full-time, going to school full-time, and trying to maintain a healthy marriage. I arrived home from school one day to find Kalenn in tears. She had been reconciling our bank account and was overwhelmed to discover that we didn't have nearly enough money to pay for rent, groceries, and impending tuition payments—even though we'd been surviving on ramen noodles! As I witnessed Kalenn's panic, something shifted inside me. I had done the math and concluded that I was not going to become a doctor. I was resolved to find a better way.

At that time Kalenn and I were attending community classes designed to strengthen new marriages. In the fifth class, we heard from a successful local businessman who spoke on basic finance and budgeting. He also mentioned real estate investing. I listened intently to his presentation and felt strongly that I should speak with him afterward. I approached him and confessed that I knew almost nothing about real estate investing, but I wanted to learn. He recommended a hard-to-find book that I tracked down and read within three days. Although I could tell that much of the information was dated, it detailed how many American millionaires had made their money in real estate.

That was enough for me; I had found my path. I just needed to do something about it. When I told my wife that I had decided to become a real estate investor, she responded, "Well, that's a funny major!"

ONE INTUITION LEADS TO 407 DEALS

I began studying everything I could find on the subject and interviewing as many people as possible. In April 2003, after another hectic day of morning classes and afternoon telemarketing, I was on my way home and felt an intuition to take a different route. I did so and stumbled across a small bungalow-style home with a "For Sale by Owner" sign in the front yard. I stopped my car and approached the house. That moment is forever etched in my mind. The sky was a beautiful blue, brushed by distant clouds. Strangely, it was snowing lightly, and the snow was falling sideways. It felt to me as if the odd weather were some kind of sign.

I walked up to the front door, feeling extremely nervous and not having a clue what I was going to say or do. I had found a pad of paper and a pen in my car, which I carried along with me; I thought it would make me look more "official."

The owner opened the door, and I explained that I was interested in her home. As she gave me a quick tour, I did my best to sound knowledgeable, though I was fairly clueless. After the tour I inquired about her asking price. She was asking $110,000. That sounded pretty good to me. "Would you consider $100,000?" I proposed hesitantly. "No!" she snapped in return. "Okay, I'll buy it for $110,000, then," I replied.

I left in a daze, unsure about what had just transpired. I arrived home and told my wife. Gratefully, she was supportive—after an extended period of hyperventilating and freaking out. A month later, we were the proud owners of our first home. We lived in it for a couple of years, put some work into it, then sold it for a $54,000 profit. Although I was too inexperienced at the time to realize it, we had bought the home at a significant discount. In other words, we made our money when we bought the home, not from mere appreciation, which is a key point for future reference.

I still remember driving home in a daze after depositing the check from the new owner of the bungalow. I was amazed. In one transaction I had made twice the amount I would make in an entire year at my full-time job. We had solved our immediate problems and my wife felt secure. Most important, I had just taken my first steps toward financial independence, and I was high on the feeling.

That first transaction turned lights on inside of me that I had never seen before—I was hooked. I knew that if I could do it once, I could do it again. It led to 407 profitable real estate deals to date that I've been personally involved in, as well as a number of blunders, which I'm now qualified to help you avoid. Through my successes and failures—the "school of hard knocks"—I developed the Strait Path system, which has created millions of dollars of wealth for hundreds of families.

Now, I spend my life teaching others how they can enjoy the same success, while continuing to invest in more real estate than ever before. I built Real Estate Investment Companies (REIC) because I was making so much money in real estate that many family members and friends were asking me what I was doing. I knew I needed to create a way to share my knowledge and system with others. I tell people, "You don't have to stick your head in a garbage can to know if it stinks." You don't have to spend years and throw away thousands of dollars making the same mistakes I have made. You can avoid "broad and crooked" paths and financial pitfalls.

The Strait Path system has been tried and perfected through hundreds of transactions. Its fruits are real, tangible, and incontrovertible. It works in every market. When properly applied, it has never lost anyone a single penny over time. It is the straightest and surest path to real estate wealth available to most investors. Furthermore, it can be applied by *every* individual, no matter the circumstances. From college students with no job history or credit to bankruptcy filers, the system has solutions for every possible scenario, complete with detailed, step-by-step instructions.

To clarify, while I do claim that the Strait Path system is the *best* form of real estate investing, the system isn't absolutely flawless or completely hassle free. Like anything, it has its challenges. Things don't always work out as planned. However, on the whole it eliminates the risk of unforeseen circumstances far better than any other system I have ever encountered.

I invite you to join me and hundreds of others on that path and create the financial independence that you crave. You can beat the statistics and be one of the few that lives a life of peace, security, happiness, fulfillment, and contribution. With that target fixed in your mind, the Strait Path system is your arrow. Follow it precisely and I guarantee you'll hit the bull's-eye, every time.

Before you get started on the path, however, it's critical that you proceed with the right mind-set.

The Crucial Mental Shift: Overcoming America's Broken Financial Paradigm

> "I noticed that my poor dad was poor not because of the amount of money he earned, which was significant, but because of his thoughts and actions. As a young boy, having two fathers, I became acutely aware of being careful which thoughts I chose to adopt as my own. Whom should I listen to—my rich dad or my poor dad?"
>
> —Robert Kiyosaki

You're probably anxious to get to the details of the Strait Path system. However, I urge you not to underestimate the importance of this chapter—your entire success as a Strait Path investor depends on it. To put it more plainly, if you struggle with the concepts presented in this chapter, I discourage you from using this investment system. Strait Path real estate is intended for people with a specific worldview, much of which goes against the grain of popular culture and investment advice. Furthermore, success on the Strait Path is predicated on your ability to persevere through challenges, which is a function of your mind-set. For many, utilizing this system requires a fundamental paradigm shift. It is a hurdle that often bounces people off the path. But for those who can make the shift, doors are opened, barriers collapse, and the road to prosperity is made clear.

America has a monumental problem—for which Strait Path real estate offers the solution. The problem is what I call the "accumulation mind-set." We've been entrenched in this flawed, Industrial Age mind-set for the last century. Corporations with vested interests bombard us with "evidence" of why we should accept and perpetuate it. The media drowns us with one-sided advice designed to promote it. Thus, we have developed a certain retirement worldview dictating how we define "safe" and "risky" investment strategies.

THE 401(K) TRAP

Specifically, we've been trained to think that the road to retirement is to work at the same job for thirty years, contribute to a 401(k), IRA, or other qualified plan, diversify our portfolio, and wait, counting on the market to bring us the returns we need to build a large enough "nest egg" that will allow us to live off the interest.

This system—this accumulation mind-set—is broken and outdated. It hasn't worked for the vast majority of workers. Furthermore, its chances for success only get dimmer with time as the financial crisis deepens and we continue to live longer. Even if we assume perfect market conditions, will traditional savings plans be enough? Almost everyone I pose that question to answers "No." If that's the case, then why do we continue contributing to something that we already know is broken? (If you question whether traditional investing is broken, read this article that explains why your 401(k) may be your riskiest investment: www.401khoax.com/why-your-401k-is-risky/.)

For most, the annual retirement income will provide only a small fraction of what is needed to maintain the current standard of living during retirement. When I do these calculations for most people I meet

Exercise: Will Your 401(k) Be Enough?

1. Write down how much of your income you consume annually for living expenses and recreation.
   Total Expenses (A): _____

2. Write down how much you currently have in 401(k)s, IRAs, annuities, or mutual funds.
   Total Savings (B): _____

3. Next, write down the best scenario of what you think those funds will grow to by the time you reach age sixty-five.
   Projected Total Savings (C): _____

4. Multiply your final projected number (C) by 5 percent to get the annual dividend you'll receive at retirement. (C × .05 = D)
   Projected Annual Retirement Dividend (D): _____

5. Now calculate what percentage of your current standard of living that dividend will support. (D ÷ A = E) Convert E into a percentage by multiplying by 100.
   Retirement Income as a Percentage of Your Current Standard of Living (E): _____

with—and even when I add Social Security to the total—it's realized that they'll be forced to live off a third or less of what they have been accustomed to their whole lives. Furthermore, when you add inflation to the calculations, the projections look even grimmer. It's clear to see why I call this system broken; it's simply impossible for most people to accumulate enough money to make it work.

THE PITFALL OF HOME EQUITY

In addition to stuffing money into risky products, another problem with the accumulation mind-set is that it promotes misguided strategies for paying off homes. Specifically, accumulators often get ten- or fifteen-year mortgages and attempt to pay off their homes from their job incomes alone. While I do advocate that people pay off their homes, there is a much better way of doing so than is traditionally taught.

When we rush to pay off our homes, we build more equity, but then we allow more of our assets to lie dormant. Suppose your home is worth $300,000 and you owe $200,000. Having $100,000 of home equity might feel good, and it might look good on your balance sheet. But what good is it doing for you? What return is it generating for you? If we go by the seventy-five-year inflation average, your return on home equity is −3.6 percent. (Source: ftp://ftp.bls.gov/pub/special.requests/cpi/cpiai.txt). What difference would it make in your family finances if we could take that $100,000 from a −3.6 percent return and shift it to a more than 50 percent average annual return? If you have even $1 of home equity, what are you earning on that bank account of bricks? You're not earning anything—in fact, you're losing.

You may be thinking that you want to pay off your home, so allow me to clarify. I'm a firm believer that everyone should pay off his or her home. I'm not telling you that you shouldn't do so. I *am* inviting you to consider the order in which you pay it off. With a slight shift in your thinking, you can actually pay off your home quicker and have potentially hundreds of thousands, and even millions, of dollars left over.

In my experience, most people who pay off their homes before reaching retirement end up selling or refinancing the home in order to live anyway. They tied up their greatest asset and therefore had nothing to invest. I call this premature retirement. What's the point of paying off your home if you haven't yet built up enough residual income? Why would you shove those dollars under the equity mattress without leveraging them first? If you're really serious about paying off your home, then I encourage you to use the Strait Path system for five years and you'll be able to pay it off a few times over. Again, it's not an either/or, but rather an issue of timing.

Of course, there are many who continue to teach the broken, outdated advice regarding accumulation vehicles and home equity. And the argument could be made that accumulation doesn't work because people aren't saving. (See this article: www.doctorhousingbubble.com/american-savings-americans-save-an-average-of-392-per-year-total-consumer-debt-is-over-25-trillion-the-dark-knight-of-debt/.) That may be true but it doesn't change the fact. I'm all for disciplined saving and financial responsibility. But I reject the idea that financial independence comes from handing off our money to institutions and praying that they'll take good care of it. The practice of putting money into accounts that we don't understand and that we have little control of is silly. Depending on a nebulous, volatile, and fickle "market" to secure our financial future is gambling, not investing. Competing with inflation means that most people are lucky to earn one or two percent annual returns on their retirement funds.

It's obvious that something more practical and likely to succeed is needed. We need a system that encourages more personal responsibility and provides more control and safety to individuals. We need tools for outpacing inflation, beating burdensome taxation, transcending market volatility, and producing passive income. What's really needed is a fundamental shift in mind-set, rather than more or different products and strategies. This critical shift occurs as individuals choose the creative power of abundance over the limiting mind-set of scarcity. It occurs as we learn to *create* opportunity, rather than wait for the market to take care of us. It manifests as exponential growth as we learn to make money work for us, rather than working for our money. It happens as we take direct responsibility for our financial health and realize that we as individuals are our best investment. There's no hot stock or trendy mutual fund that's going to give you lasting wealth. No "expert" or institution cares more about your money than you do. You are the only one who can take charge and make your dreams a reality.

REIC Investors Share Their Experience: David and Kelly

"Being first-time investors, we've definitely had some insecurities along the way. After talking with Kris and others in the program, we have been able to develop a more complete and long-term perspective of real estate investing that has helped us feel more secure and be more optimistic. Kris truly exemplifies an 'abundance mentality' that helps one overcome the 'scarcity mentality' that so many of us who were raised in the rat race suffer with.

"Being involved with this group has already changed our lives. We now live in a much nicer home and have changed the way we think about money and investing. Our money management has improved, and even how we carry out our daily activities has changed. The idea of investing is now real and happening for us, and we have a great hope for a very bright future.

"With this program we have constant mentoring and support from expert and successful investors. Also, our investment properties are in the local area, which makes them much easier to manage. Our children are watching us as we do the program and learning the concepts of money and investing. We have great hopes that they will be able to lead a much better life than we have so far."

To provide further context into how important this concept is, I don't offer real estate as an end-all, be-all wealth creation vehicle. Despite my confidence in my system, I understand that it ultimately depends on the individuals using it. And I can't stress enough how challenging real estate investing can be. If you're thinking of this system like most people think of a 401(k)—as something you just throw money at and forget about—it's not going to work for you. In other words, it's less about tangible real estate and more about the real estate between your ears. When one understands the investor mind-set of personal responsibility, innovation, and tenacity, then real estate becomes a powerful tool. It offers much greater control, flexibility, and potential returns than most other methods of wealth creation. But these doors can only be opened with the key of the right mind-set.

My hunch is that most Americans intuitively understand that the mainstream retirement thinking doesn't work; they simply don't know what else to do. In the absence of options, they default to convention. The potential options they *are* aware of appear to be risky, so they "play it safe"—which automatically equates to playing small.

The unfortunate reality is that this safety is largely a perception. Just try to tell the sixty-year-old who lost half of her retirement account values in 2008 that mutual funds and IRAs are safe. The government reported that household net worth plummeted by $11.2 trillion in 2008 alone. In January 2009 the *Wall Street Journal* reported that "About 50 million Americans have 401(k) plans, which have $2.5 trillion in total assets, estimates the Employee Benefit Research Institute in Washington. In the twelve months following the stock market's peak in October 2007, more than $1 trillion worth of stock value held in 401(k)s and other 'defined-contribution' plans was wiped out, according to the Boston College research center. If individual retirement accounts, which consist largely of money rolled over from 401(k)s, are taken into account, about $2 trillion of stock value evaporated." The article concluded bluntly, "Even if workers follow the golden rules of 401(k) investing—saving early and diligently, holding a broadly diversified investment mix, never tapping their savings until retirement—their success can still depend largely on the luck of the stock-market draw." (Source: http://online.wsj.com/article/SB123137714796462913.html).

Meanwhile, Strait Path investors continue to produce safe, stable, and lucrative returns. Many of them will technically be able to retire within ten years, and some much sooner. The core difference between accumulators and investors is that accumulators try to create retirement from one or two household incomes, while investors create assets that work for them; the investors have multiple income streams to draw from and leverage. Each property you purchase on the Strait Path works for your retirement. If you can get ten or more homes working for you, you won't have to work a nine-to-five job. The key is learning to work smarter, not harder.

> **Calculate and Compare**
>
> We've created an online tool to help you calculate the net results of a traditional retirement plan versus the Strait Path real estate plan. Visit www.straitpathrealestate.com now to calculate your plan and compare the results side by side.

Twenty-three years ago, one of our investors, Ron, did an internship with a manufacturing facility while in college. He liked it so much that he ended up taking a job with them as an engineer. Five years later, a married man with children and responsibilities, Ron began thinking of his future. Having very little guidance and not knowing what else to do, he started saving in the company 401(k). For eighteen years he saved diligently. At its highest point his retirement account totaled $247,000. He was also paying extra mortgage payments with the intention of having his home paid off before retirement.

At the age of forty-four, he began analyzing the numbers and realized that his 401(k) wasn't going to be enough to retire on, even if everything went well. He also realized that, at his current rate, he wouldn't be able to pay off his home by retirement age. Feeling trapped, doomed to work until he was sixty-seven or even older, he began searching for other investment vehicles. He started reading mind-shifting books from authors such as Dale Carnegie and Napoleon Hill. He knew there had to be a different, better way than he had been taught—he just had to find it.

His search came to fruition when he learned about Strait Path real estate. After performing due diligence, he was ready to act. He refinanced his home to extract $130,000 of equity, then purchased four investment properties within eleven months, giving him a total real estate portfolio of $1.1 million. Between when he first started applying the Strait Path system and now, his net worth has increased by $250,000. *In three years he has made more than what it took him eighteen years to make in his 401(k).* Furthermore, his assets are now collateralized, and they provide an immediate and ongoing cash flow of $500 per month, not factoring in the amounts he's received in down payments. And if the economy continues to worsen, he can still derive an income from his real estate.

The sad part of Ron's story is that he didn't liquidate his 401(k) until it had dwindled from $247,000 to $130,000; while the economy was crashing, he was still researching and trying to make decisions. That's $117,000 that could have been used to purchase more real estate. Fortunately, however, he's now in a much safer and profitable position than he was three years ago—despite his awful losses in the market. Also, he did liquidate his remaining $130,000 to purchase additional real estate.

Ron says that he now has an entirely new outlook on life. He sees many more possibilities than he ever has. He feels much more in control, rather than, in his words, "being pulled by the nose in the system." He feels empowered to be the creator of his life. Though at times he wished he could turn the clock back, he's drawn his line in the sand and is moving forward.

Another of our clients, Chris, was also captured by the 401(k) trap in his first job out of college. Learning the virtue of saving as a young man, he thought it was the prudent thing to do. Saving *is* a virtue—when you understand the savings vehicle. Unfortunately, he put his savings in a traditional retirement account that he knew little about. He and his wife, Shanna, were pleased to see their account rise in the first year. The second year, however, was a different story; their account plummeted and their gains were erased. They began questioning whether the standard approach would serve them long-term.

But with little knowledge of other options, they pressed forward for about fifteen years longer. Throughout these years, they discussed the idea of real estate investing but could never agree on the strategy. Shanna pushed Chris to pursue rentals, but he dragged his feet because he feared the common headaches associated with rentals, such as receiving annoying maintenance phone calls in the middle of the night and managing lousy tenants. In response, he suggested flipping properties, mistakenly thinking that this would mitigate their risk.

In 2008 Chris and Shanna learned about the Strait Path. Using cash they had in bank accounts, they quickly purchased their first two homes. Soon after, they refinanced their home and used the equity to purchase two more investments. Then, they partnered with a friend to purchase yet another property in the same year. These five investments brought in more than $15,000 in tenant down payments, immediately increased their net worth by more than $300,000, and produce a positive monthly cash flow of $1,165.

At its highest point—and after more than fifteen years—their 401(k) totaled about $100,000. In 2008 it tumbled to $65,000. Though they want to liquidate the account and use the proceeds to buy more real estate, they are prohibited from doing so as long as Chris is employed by his company. When I first met them, their net worth stood at about $600,000. Within less than a year, that figure has leaped to about $2.1 million after they engaged on the Strait Path.

Their increased wealth is one thing; what it allows them to do is another. Chris is passionate about helping people increase their resilience, their ability to manage opposition successfully. He and Shanna have a dream of building a foundation with this focus—and the Strait Path provides the funding for that dream, which would not have been possible had they stayed on the worn-out, traditional retirement path.

Understand this: Blindly throwing money at funds, accounts, and products that you don't understand, that you can't control, that lock up your principal, that offer no collateral, that depend upon market cooperation, that eat up your money with administration fees (which are often hidden), that provide poor exit strategies, that are subject to government change and control, and that cause you to relinquish personal responsibility is *not* investing. It is gambling. If you really want to succeed, if your retirement and your dreams are to become realities, then you must reject the accumulation mind-set and embrace the investor mind-set.

WHAT IS AN INVESTOR?

My definition of a successful investor may surprise you because of its simplicity. Successful investors are certainly motivated, hardworking, talented, wise, and patient. They have sophisticated knowledge and are dedicated to lifelong learning. They enjoy insights that others don't share. They have the ability to create plans and the discipline to stick with them. However, there's one key that makes a successful investor and that encompasses every other necessary attribute. *A successful investor is someone who knows how to accomplish something that most people cannot do.* Essentially, investors are problem solvers; they possess a wholly different mind-set than most people have. The financially successful learn to see an abundance of options in every situation, while those who struggle see limited options.

"A resourceful person can see opportunity when others only see obstacles."—Garrett Gunderson, author, *Killing Sacred Cows*

Investors, like entrepreneurs, operate in environments that may seem negative, volatile, and risky. Their task is to formulate solutions that overcome fear and risk and create value for others in sustainable ways. They must find success where others see only failure. They must persist when others give up.

People often mistakenly believe that wealth is merely a function of participating in the right opportunity. While it may be true that an opportunity may be the vehicle to create wealth, I am convinced that wealth is ultimately a function of how we think and act. Simply put, some people cultivate poor thoughts and habits, while others cultivate wealthy thoughts and habits. You have the power to choose how you respond to life's difficulties. You have the power to create opportunity. You have the power to become a successful investor.

One of our investors, Edee, has a powerful story of the freedom that the investor mind-set creates. As a mother of six children, she felt stuck in their small twin home. The small backyard wasn't fenced and they lived on a busy street, so she was constantly worried about her children playing outside. After learning the Strait Path system, she applied it to completely change their situation. First, she sold her home using our seller-financing program (Compassionate Financing) and received a $7,000 down payment plus monthly payments that generated a positive cash flow of $300. Edee then found a perfect home in her dream neighborhood on a cul-de-sac and with a huge, fenced backyard. Not only does the home have enough bedrooms for each of her children, it also has an apartment, which she rents out for $700 per month. Between this rent and the rent she receives from her first home, they essentially pay nothing for housing expenses. The root of her lifestyle change was a change in mind-set and the courage to act on the knowledge she had gained.

Accumulators often develop the scarcity mind-set, which dictates that resources and choices are limited, and that wealth is a zero-sum game. They hoard from fear that there won't be enough material resources to meet their needs. Such fear leads them to embrace illusory security rather than create opportunity. It leads them to make poor investment decisions, such as buying high on greed and selling low on fear. They try to grow their retirement funds from finite dollars, rather than multiplying the effect of those dollars.

In contrast, investors have an abundance mind-set. They understand that resources can be made unlimited through human ingenuity and

The Accumulation Mind-Set	The Investor Mind-Set
• Tends toward scarcity mind-set by trying to grow wealth from finite dollars	• Tends toward abundance mind-set by creating exponential wealth
• Accumulates cash by saving over time	• Multiplies net worth and builds residual income by buying real assets
• Saves in unsecured, uncollateralized vehicles	• Collateralizes assets (i.e., real estate)
• Subject to markets, inflation, taxation, and other wealth-eroding factors	• Leverages knowledge and control to create relative immunity
• Depends on corporations and "experts" for financial success (abdicates personal responsibility)	• Depends on self for financial success (accepts personal responsibility)
• Feels entitled to benefits, security, and success	• Feels called to serve and produce
• Thinks security comes from money	• Knows that security comes from applied knowledge
• Leads to unhappiness by being beholden to golden handcuffs	• Leads to freedom
• Waits for opportunity	• Creates opportunity
• Thinks high returns come from high risks	• Understands that high returns come from mitigating risk

innovation. They understand that exchange creates wealth for all parties, not just for one at the expense of others. Rather than hoarding cash, they build assets, which then produce perpetual income streams. They overcome the emotions of fear and greed through the knowledge that opportunity can always be created.

TWO WAYS TO DEVELOP THE INVESTOR MIND-SET

There are obviously many ways to experience the paradigm shift I speak of. But I want to get you quickly to the details of the Strait Path system, so I'll briefly mention two here: embracing the possibility attitude and living the law of now. Together, these two concepts open you up to thinking in new ways, and then give you the courage to act on that thinking.

Possibility Attitude

"The last of the human freedoms is to choose one's attitude in any given set of circumstances—to choose one's own way."
—Viktor Frankl, psychiatrist and concentration camp survivor

"Positive attitude" has been discussed by so many authors, speakers, and coaches that it has become cliché. But people talk about it so much for a reason—it really is true. Happiness is a choice, not a circumstance or event. Your own happiness is up to you. Positive people tend to attract more of what they want in life. Complainers see negativity, and that focus creates and attracts more negativity. Cultivating a positive attitude helps you see opportunities in challenges. It makes you focus on solutions, rather than problems, which is the hallmark of an investor. *You will become wealthy to the degree that you can see an abundance of options.* Wealthy people see limitless options; poor people see limited options.

The reality is this: Almost anything is possible with the right attitude. This is why I refer to this concept as "possibility" attitude, which means to always be open to the possibility of any form of progression and increased prosperity. Negative people by default limit their options: "How could I ever afford that? I'm just not smart enough. I'm not educated enough. I don't have the right connections." Sound familiar? You can fill in the "not enough" blank with a lot of things that are commonly expressed.

In contrast, positive possibilities are expressed far less often, such as, "I know it's possible for me to get the funding I need for that dream business. There's a way—I just have to find it. I can do anything I want if I put my mind to it."

My friend Justin has had incredible success with applying the possibility attitude. His father was an airline pilot, and he was raised with the quote "Attitude determines altitude" plastered throughout his home. He had read many books, listened to audio CDs, and attended many courses on self-improvement and self-empowerment, so he understood the mentality.

However, in 2008 he experienced a number of trials that made it difficult to stay positive. Two semesters shy of getting his bachelor's degree, he realized that his field of study held no promise. Furthermore, his business was failing, *and* he had a second child on the way. Negative thinking began creeping into and affecting his life. Though he had the knowledge, he wasn't applying it. When he attended one of our seminars, one key principle stuck out to him: Knowledge is meaningless unless it is applied. He rededicated himself to controlling his thought processes and attitude.

He sat down and made a list of goals, and then wrote them on his mirror so he could refer to them often. His two overriding goals were to succeed through real estate and to be earning a certain amount within a year. He had no idea how he was going to do it, especially given the economic turmoil. He had no technical resume experience for what he wanted to do. Despite all this, deep down he knew it was possible.

He started by applying a principle he had learned from Napoleon Hill, which is to work for free—volunteer—to provide value in ways and in positions that will help one's personal quest. He approached Steve Earl, the CEO of Real Estate Investment Companies, and asked how he could help. Steve put him to work and we quickly saw what he was capable of. For example, we had a home that hadn't sold for ten months, and Steve asked Justin to sell it. Justin was given this challenge at the beginning of December, and he set a goal of selling it by Christmas. It closed on December 23. Steve gave him another property to sell, which he promptly sold within three days, collecting $7,000 down and getting Steve's full asking price on the monthly rent.

Within ninety days of Justin's writing down his goal, Steve sat Justin down and offered him a position to manage our seller-financing program. Steve wrote on a piece of paper a few details regarding Justin's job duties, and then finished by writing a salary figure. Justin was astounded to see that it was within $400 of the goal he had set for himself. He keeps that paper as a reminder of the reality of the possibility attitude.

But Justin didn't stop there; he has continued to shine in his role. We had hired another individual, whom Justin managed, to handle our seller-financing program in another city. This individual was struggling, not having closed a sale in sixty days. Justin decided to spend a full training day with him, and Justin implanted the thought into this employee's mind that they would sell a contract that very day. They began going through old call logs together and were able to set up an appointment with one potential client, but the meeting went horribly, even turning confrontational. Still, Justin was not discouraged. They kept at it and scheduled another meeting. This time, within thirty minutes the client was sold on the Compassionate Financing program. They drove to the home and the client fell in love with it. They followed him to his credit union where they picked up the option consideration fee, and the deal was finalized the next day. Justin has repeated that exact scenario on three more occasions. Because of Justin's positive attitude and excellent training help, our other seller-financing manager who initially struggled is now successful.

Justin didn't have a resume brimming with experience. What he had was a possibility attitude and the commitment to persevere in spite of challenges; he thought like a proactive investor, rather than a reactive accumulator.

The Law of Now

> "Do not wait. The time will never be 'just right.' Start where you stand, and work with whatever tools you may have at your command, and better tools will be found as you go along."
> —Napoleon Hill, author, *Think and Grow Rich*

A possibility attitude without action is like an engine without gas; it can never get you to your desired destination. No matter what has happened in your past, no matter what you fear in the future, at some point you must pull the trigger and act in the now. There is magic and power in confident decision making and conscious, forthright action.

Ironically, it's the *start* of any endeavor that stops most people. Fearful of making the wrong decisions and following through with misguided action, they are paralyzed. But successful investors are bold decision makers and action takers. Those who take firm action and occasionally make wrong decisions succeed far more often than those who never make a wrong decision—except to remain stagnant through indecision and inaction. Orrin Woodward, coauthor of *Launching a Leadership Revolution*, says it best: "I have learned more from bad decisions than indecision. Leaders must make the tough calls to learn and lead."

I have made thousands of decisions throughout my investing career. Although I have been wrong and I have lost out multiple times, in the long run I have always come out far ahead because I was not afraid to take action. Now that the Strait Path has been tried and tested, you have a clear advantage: you can feel even more confident and comfortable taking action than I was in my early years of investing.

Action is facilitated by learning to be present in the moment. The future is but an abstract fantasy playing out in your mind now, and the past is comprised of your memories, which exist in the now. We often rely upon past experience to make better future judgments, and we envision the future in order to be prepared. There is wisdom in these practices, yet far too often the past becomes a crutch and the future becomes a roadblock. We fail to act because we fear failure, and thus we automatically secure the failure we feared.

The Law of Now says to gather all available data, make a decision, and then act immediately on the decision. Good things happen to those who take action. Even if you're headed in the wrong direction, you'll realize your error more quickly if you act in the now, rather than vacillate with indecision. We're trained to think that mistakes are bad, but entrepreneurs and investors have a completely different perspective. To them, mistakes are turned into stepping-stones that get them closer to their goals. Those who are afraid of making decisions are those who inevitably make the worst decisions because they have little practical experience to draw upon.

Living the law of now requires faith—faith in who we are as creative beings, capable of choosing our actions and responses; faith that we can learn and progress in spite of mistakes; faith in the laws of consequence. As long as we keep moving forward, acting with confidence in the now and learning from our mistakes along the way, we will get what we desire.

I have a friend who has made many investment mistakes, which have led him to bankruptcy. In the eyes of the world, he may appear to be a failure, but I know a deeper truth. I know that he is actually head and shoulders above his peers because of what he has learned by being unafraid to act. Yes, he has made mistakes, but these mistakes were born of a willingness to act while others around him criticized and stayed stagnant. He's now much more prepared to prosper than these disparagers because he understands investing at such a deeper level.

> "Don't wait until everything is just right. It will never be perfect. There will always be challenges, obstacles, and less than perfect conditions. So what. Get started now. With each step you take, you will grow stronger and stronger, more and more skilled, more and more self-confident, and more and more successful."—Mark Victor Hansen, coauthor, *The One Minute Millionaire*

Learn wisdom from the past and have hope in the future, but act in the now. Act like an investor.

DO WHAT WORKS

Aside from the things we've discussed, the real problem with the accumulation mind-set is that *it just doesn't work*. After trying to make it work for the last century—with dismal results—we're way beyond theory and personal opinion and preference. You may *prefer* to be able to hand off your money to a financial advisor and then hope that she picks the right funds, that the market cooperates with your time frame, and that inflation and administration fees won't erode your money so that you can then wake up in thirty years with a fat nest egg. You can prefer and hope, but that plan won't work.

I recently met with a mature couple who had done one of the best jobs I have ever seen in the accumulation mind-set. After working for thirty-five years they had their home paid off, which was worth about $350,000, and they had another $300,000 in 401(k)s and IRAs, for a total net worth of $650,000. After doing a few calculations, we established that they would need at least three times that to be able to retire without minimizing their current lifestyle. Unfortunately, they wanted to retire within five years. Accumulation does not work—even for those who do it "right."

If the current economic turmoil hasn't convinced you that there are serious flaws with the accumulation road to retirement, then there's probably little I can say that will change your mind. My hope, however, is that enough people are now realizing that things must change, and that the change starts with them as individuals. The question of whether accumulation works has been answered. The accumulation mind-set is losing its grip and fading into history. The relevant question now is how to practically apply the investor mind-set. And Strait Path real estate is the answer to that question.

Overview of the Strait Path System

You've heard the phrase "The devil is in the details." While it's true that many important truths can be lost and hidden within details, it's also true that too much initial detail can overwhelm people. The purpose of this chapter is to give you a brief overview of the Strait Path system in order to provide a context. Without that big-picture context, the importance of critical details within the system can be overlooked. Once the context is established, the details of the system can be understood with much greater depth as they're explained later in the book.

This chapter provides a bullet-point, bottom-line analysis. If you're a relatively knowledgeable and experienced real estate investor, you'll be able to easily identify the key components that set the Strait Path apart from other systems, and it may be all you need to get started. On the other hand, if you're inexperienced, or if you're a details person, then the system is explained in much greater detail in chapters four through seven.

To get started, consider the following analogy: Suppose that three people want to drive to Florida. One lives in Seattle, Washington, another lives in San Diego, California, and the third lives in Boston, Massachusetts. Each of them will take different routes, but they'll all end up in Florida. Real estate investing is similar. While every investor has the same general destination (long-term, sustainable wealth), not everyone can take the same path to get there. Put more precisely with regard to Strait Path real estate, each investor starts at a different place but eventually ends up on the same path.

The Strait Path system consists of four core phases: 1) plan, 2) find, 3) purchase, and 4) serve.

PHASE 1: PLAN

The purpose of this first phase is threefold: 1) to identify existing resources, 2) to outline a ten-year portfolio plan for applying and leveraging those resources within the Strait Path system, and 3) to help investors stay disciplined. The first and third elements unleash the potential of the ten-year plan. Identifying and leveraging hidden assets expedites the process, while the delayed gratification ensures that you follow through on your plan and stick with it. No ten-year plan is sufficient and effective without these components.

Identifying Existing Resources

Most people are unaware of their assets and resources that can be leveraged to produce greater income and net worth. These assets lay dormant and underutilized, resulting in lost opportunity costs. For some people, these assets may be enough to create a stable retirement in just a few years. You may be surprised by what these hidden assets are (see chapters three and four to find out). Understand that everyone has them, regardless of their circumstances. Unfortunately, few people ever recognize their potential, let alone leverage them.

Ten-Year Game Plan

Once your assets are clearly identified, the next step is to create a ten-year plan that maximizes them through real estate investing. The goal is to shift unproductive resources into areas of higher productivity. A typical—and very achievable—plan results in an investor purchasing about twenty properties and making more than $2 million within ten years. However, since everyone's situation, abilities, and desires are different, each plan is customized.

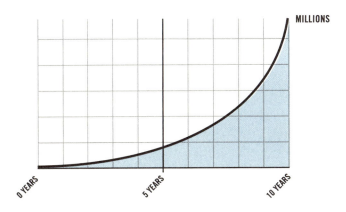

The ten-year timeline illustrates the power of Strait Path real estate. This is not a get-rich-quick scheme, nor is it a pie-in-the-sky dream. This is real. It requires serious commitment and focus. It's much more safe, profitable, and sustainable than the traditional retirement model, but those benefits are only achieved through personal responsibility.

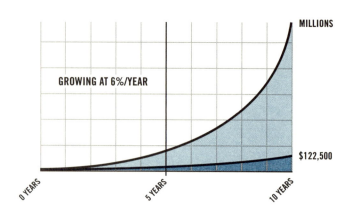

Long-Term Discipline

The Strait Path system is significantly hindered when investors are unable to stay disciplined over the course of ten years or more. When applied in its purest form, the process builds on itself to provide exponential growth. When all profits are consumed, especially in the initial stages, only linear and sporadic growth is possible.

You'll find more details on this component in chapters three and four.

Keys to Building a Portfolio Game Plan

- ▶ Identify all assets and resources, especially those that may be hidden.

- ▶ Create a clear and detailed ten-year plan to give structure to your investing.

- ▶ Stay disciplined by sticking with the system and reinvesting your profits, especially in the early years.

PHASE 2: FIND

The Strait Path system dictates that investors purchase only single-family homes with three bedrooms or more and with at least 15 percent equity. Yes, this is possible, and we prove it every day. Finding these deals is a function of four key elements: 1) knowing *where* to look, 2) knowing *how* to look, 3) knowing *what* properties to look for, and 4) speed.

Look in the Right Place

Other real estate systems teach you to look where every other investor is looking: auctions, short sales, foreclosures, fixer-uppers, etc. Since the competition is stiff in these arenas, it's extremely difficult to succeed. In contrast, at Strait Path we find properties on the largest listed-property database. When used properly, it saves tons of time and effort in the finding process.

Look in the Right Way

You'll save even more time and effort when you learn *how* to look on this database. Our system uses strategies for combing through piles of data to extract only the best deals. What's more, you don't even have to look yourself when you use realtors to locate properties for you. When you find the right realtors and train them well, you can spend your time making deals. When you search the right way, 95 percent of the finding work is done by other people.

Look for the Right Properties

In our system, though, you're not just making any deal. We're very strict about our criteria for purchasing homes. First, we purchase only single-family residences; we do not purchase townhomes, condos, duplexes, or multiplexes. Second, we never invest in homes priced above the median home price in any given area. Buying above the median home price for an area dramatically increases the risks of losing equity from market volatility and of being unable to resell. But the Strait Path system works in any market. Since we buy only the most wanted real estate (entry level up to the median price), we're far less affected by market swings, and we always have a market for our homes no matter how bad the market is. Third, we only buy homes in livable condition. We want to put the least amount of time, effort, and money into our properties, so we avoid homes that need a lot of repairs before they can be sold. This doesn't mean that our homes are perfect—they may be dated and worn. In fact, ugly but livable houses often produce huge cash flows. But they must be in good enough condition that we can find tenants/potential buyers for them; we don't waste our time and energy on fixer-uppers.

The Power of Speed

Because we use the most popular property database to locate potential properties, speed is necessarily the essence of our finding system. We're usually one or two days ahead of the competition on the properties we find, which is a rarity in the highly competitive market of short sales and foreclosures. Speed is achieved in three ways: 1) being prepared to purchase homes beforehand, 2) being the first to find deals, and 3) having an efficient style of negotiation.

Great deals are, quite literally, here today and gone tomorrow, which means that we must be prepared to act on them immediately. A purchase plan, including being prequalified by a mortgage broker (depending on the circumstances), is put in place before we ever start looking for properties. Then, our tailored finding system allows us to get to the best deals before anyone else. We qualify our finds as viable deals, and then act on them immediately. Negotiating is also a critical aspect of speed. Traditional negotiations take days, and sometimes weeks. Our system eliminates the common back-and-forth dialogue and seals the deal the same day, before other offers can come in. In short, we win because we're extraordinarily fast!

You'll find more details on the Strait Path finding system in chapter five.

Keys to Finding and Securing the Best Deals

- Be prepared to purchase before you start looking.
- Avoid competition from investors by staying away from common arenas such as short sales and foreclosures, and instead, look for properties solely on the Multiple Listing Service.
- Leverage the time and resources of realtors by having them find deals for you.
- Purchase only single-family homes priced at or below the median home price for the area to secure immunity from market volatility.
- Purchase only homes in livable condition and that do not require major repairs before you can sell them. Let your tenants make home improvements (see Phase 4: Serve Through Compassionate Financing).
- Use the focused search system to identify deals with at least 15 percent equity, and then get to them before anyone else. Speed is of the essence.
- Eliminate wasted time in the negotiation stage by cutting to the chase and avoiding tedious counteroffers.

PHASE 3: PURCHASE

Real Estate Investment Companies employs a unique purchasing system and proprietary financing formula. It enables us to help people with average jobs and credit do something that few lending institutions can accomplish, which is to leverage the maximum number of investment homes onto a person's credit. Our complex formula considers various banks and ratios, and then combines with our real estate system to achieve this. Your success during this phase is determined by three primary factors: 1) using the right broker, 2) selecting the right loans, and 3) managing your debt-to-income ratio. If you are unable to secure traditional financing for credit reasons, Strait Path has creative options for getting around that issue.

Use the Right Mortgage Broker

The banking industry is complicated. It requires specific training and cutting-edge information to stay abreast of all your banking options. Our clients are able to acquire multiple homes because we've learned the secrets of the lending industry. Banks decide whether or not to fund investment properties based on how many mortgages you already have on your credit, how quickly they were acquired, what banks they are with, how your file was submitted, and what you are doing with your properties, just to name a few criteria. We've learned how to maximize your ability to acquire the most investments possible. Our formula for leveraging several homes on your credit requires us to use banks in specific combinations, so that each additional bank will follow and accept your next investment purchase. And since we're looking ten years into the future, we protect your ability to purchase more homes in the future. For do-it-yourself investors, the key is to find the right mortgage broker who understands how to finance multiple properties on one person's credit.

Select the Right Loans

Maximizing investor portfolios also requires us to be strategic about which loans we choose. For example, if your goal is to pay a home off over time and you secured a thirty-year or fifteen-year fixed loan to do it, that strategy would cap out very soon and you would qualify for only a fraction of the loans that you would be eligible for if you had used more flexible loans. These specialized loans capitalize on the best cash flows and overall profits for your portfolio.

Also, maximizing the benefits of our formula requires that investors learn how to become profit conscious, rather than rate conscious. Higher interest rates can make investors more money than lower rates. Because the goal is to finance as many homes as possible, each additional property may be funded at a higher interest rate. Paying higher interest rates to particular banks enables us to purchase twice the investment properties as compared to what we could do if we went with the banks with the lowest rates.

Optimize Debt-to-Income Ratios Through Compassionate Financing

One major factor that determines your success in the loan process is your debt-to-income ratio. The higher your debt is relative to your income, the less likely you are to get additional loans. Through Compassionate Financing, our proprietary hybrid rent-to-own system, you can collect between $300 and $600 per month more than is possible through renting out properties. This offsets the debt incurred by additional loans and increases your ability to purchase additional investment properties. This is opposed to renting, where your debt-to-income ratio worsens with each transaction, and usually kills your ability to grow your portfolio after you've purchased a couple of homes.

Creative Financing

One of the best aspects of Strait Path real estate is that it can be applied by virtually anyone, no matter his or her history and the state of his or her credit. For those who cannot get approved for traditional financing, there are two ways to finance investment properties: "sandwich financing" and partnering. *Sandwich financing* is securing a property under favorable seller-financing terms, and then turning around and financing the property to an end buyer—using Compassionate Financing—for a profit. *Partnering* is identifying people who can get approved for traditional financing, and then creating an arrangement where you both can profit. For example, you find properties and get them under contract, and your partner finances them on his or her credit, and you split the profits. Parents, in-laws, siblings, coworkers, bosses, and friends are all great candidates for partnering—especially as they see you succeeding.

In the meantime, you should be doing everything you can to increase your ability to get traditional financing. I cover the complexities of purchasing investment properties in greater detail in chapter six.

Keys to Purchasing Multiple Investment Properties

- ▶ Use the right mortgage broker who understands how to finance multiple homes on one person's credit.

- ▶ Become profit conscious, rather than rate conscious. Go with the banks that let you buy the most real estate, not those with the best rates.

- ▶ Use specialized loan programs, which allow you to maximize the number of homes on your credit.

- ▶ Use Compassionate Financing to optimize your debt-to-income ratio.

- ▶ If you're unable to get approved for traditional financing, use creative financing options to get started while you're improving your ability to secure traditional loans.

PHASE 4: SERVE THROUGH COMPASSIONATE FINANCING

Every component of the Strait Path system is important, but Compassionate Financing is the engine that makes it all run. Compassionate Financing is a rent-to-own program similar to lease options and other seller-financing programs. It's a powerful and highly profitable system for the following reasons: 1) it incorporates the best elements of lease options while eliminating the flaws, 2) it relieves investors of the time and effort required to maintain rentals, 3) it generates much higher profits than either rentals or flipping, and 4) it provides substantial benefits to tenants.

Leasing: The Benefits Without the Flaws

Almost everyone wants to own a home, rather than rent, but there are many who are unable to qualify for traditional financing. A lease option gives renters the opportunity to purchase a home within a specified period of time and if certain conditions are met. Renters like the lease option because it offers a gateway to home ownership. Investors like the lease option because it allows them to collect an option consideration (down payment) and receive a higher lease payment than they would otherwise receive in rent.

Unfortunately, lease-to-own options are risky for many homebuyers because of the way in which greedy, misguided investors apply them. These investors collect large, nonrefundable option considerations and stipulate a short time period for the lessees to purchase the home. Then, when their tenants are unable to get traditional financing, they boot them out of the home and begin the process all over again with someone else. Many actually hope their tenants will be unable to purchase the home. One of the key elements of sustainable investing is service to individuals, communities, and society. But this uncompassionate type of investing does not exist to serve, and is therefore unsustainable. It might make a handful of unscrupulous investors good money, but it weakens communities in the long run.

In contrast, the end goal of Compassionate Financing is for tenants to purchase our homes. We deliberately do everything in our power to ensure that they do, even providing financial coaches and assistance with credit repair. We've implemented a number of revolutionary elements into our contracts to reduce risk and create a more equitable arrangement between investors and tenants. Interestingly enough, this approach typically makes us more money than most investors who use traditional lease options earn. It's a triple-win scenario—we win, our tenants win, and the community wins.

Potential for Much Higher Profits Than Through Rentals

Compassionate Financing offers much higher profits than traditional rentals. Its benefits include the following:

- You receive anywhere from $50 to a few hundred dollars more per month than rentals.

- You collect a down payment (technically an "option consideration") up front that equates to an extra $100 to $300 per month over the course of the contract.

- You don't pay $75 to $150 per month in property management fees.

- You never have to pay for repairs, which can add up to an extra $50 to $250 per month with rentals, if not more.

Those first four bullet points increase your profits by $300 to $800 per month as compared to rentals. These final three points result in tens of thousands of dollars of increased profits over time:

- You can sell the property on the back end for at least its current market value, which is often not possible with rentals because tenants often do not maintain rental properties, causing them to decrease in value. Typically, if an investor chooses to sell a rental property after renting it out for a couple of years, he or she must either spend a lot of money to fix it up or knock 10 percent or more off the asking price to attract buyers.

- It lowers your debt-to-income ratio relative to rentals, which means that you can purchase more properties.

- You save 6 percent on realtor fees when the home sells.

No Property Maintenance

Unlike rentals, with Compassionate Financing there is no property maintenance for investors, since the contract stipulates that tenants are responsible for all maintenance. The only time and effort involved is in marketing the property, screening tenants, and putting contracts in place.

Service to Tenants and the Community

The best part of Compassionate Financing is that it provides tenants huge benefits that they cannot get in any other way. While it frees you from having to repair toilets, it gives tenants the opportunity to make improvements and feel as if they're really creating a home environment, which is difficult for renters to achieve. Tenants have the feeling of control and ownership while they are buying time to improve their credit. They can build equity much faster than they can with conventional financing. They can acquire seasoned loans since they are living in the home before purchasing it. They can take advantage of the opportunity of home ownership with a relatively small amount of money. And with our system, it's almost a guarantee that they will, in fact, be able to purchase the home. Furthermore, we encourage investors to give tenants an equity bonus when they purchase the home.

You'll find all the details on the Compassionate Financing system in chapter seven.

Keys to Compassionate Financing

- By giving tenants the opportunity to purchase a home, you relieve yourself of the burden of property maintenance, decrease your risk, and increase your profits.

- ▶ You eliminate the predatory nature of lease options, as well as the risk of lost appreciation by using better contracts than standard contracts.

- ▶ You help tenants purchase homes. It serves them better and makes you more profit in the long run.

- ▶ Compassionate Financing gives tenants substantial benefits, such as the ability to make home improvements, time to improve their credit, and the opportunity to build equity. In exchange for these benefits, they are willing to pay more up front, as well as on a monthly basis.

Once you've gone through the four-phase Strait Path process (plan, find, purchase, serve) with one home, things really start to get exciting, since your success builds exponentially. The more properties you buy, the more you're able to buy. One home can easily become many over time. Once you purchase a home at a discount and it generates profits, you can leverage those profits and the accumulated equity to purchase another property, and another and another. This is what we refer to as "achieving critical mass," which is detailed in chapter eight.

ACHIEVING CRITICAL MASS

- ▶ Create the "snowball" effect through the discipline of delaying gratification and repetition.

- ▶ Create exponential growth through repetition.

- ▶ Create infinite growth through partnerships.

- ▶ Leverage your time and effort by forming a Power Team.

Obviously, the Strait Path system is much more detailed than what I have covered in this brief chapter. For now, it's important to know that the system incorporates the best aspects of almost every form of real estate, eliminates the flaws and risks of those methods, and creates an unrivaled hybrid. It generates the cash flow of rentals without requiring property maintenance. It gives you the equity of fixer-uppers without the risk. It gives you the appreciation potential of spec building without the speculative element. It helps you find discounted properties without having to deal with the competition of foreclosures and short sales.

In short, it helps you find the best deals while expending the least time and effort, reduces your risk as much as possible, serves people at a much higher level than most other systems, works in every market, and generates the highest profits in a comprehensive comparison. And speaking of comparisons, read on to see how Strait Path real estate stacks up against every other real estate system and strategy.

The Six Elements of Successful Investing: Various Methods Compared and Contrasted

I put more than $15,000 and hundreds of hours of work into my first property. I eventually sold it, making a $54,000 profit. My second property required $6,000 of repairs and about sixty hours of work, and I made over $100,000 upon selling. I never set foot on nor did I put a penny into my third property, which I sold for a $20,000 profit. Which deal yielded me the greatest return?

Even though my second deal made me $100,000, it still required a lot of time and money. My third property was the winner because it only took a few hours of my time and no money. Profit is just one aspect to consider when you're seeking the best way to invest. Granted, it's a vital factor, yet far too many people consider it to be the most important, which leads to faulty decisions. There are actually six elements of successful investing, all of which must be considered with every deal, every system, and every strategy in order to make wise investment decisions. These elements are as follows:

1. Time
2. Effort
3. Risk
4. Service
5. Market Volatility
6. Profitability

When I began creating the Strait Path system, I wasn't just looking for what would make me the most money. I wanted a system that would create the greatest profits *after considering these other core factors*. Everything else being equal, I prefer to make $20,000 in a few hours of my time versus making $40,000 with a hundred hours of my time. I don't care how lucrative a potential opportunity is—if it's highly risky, I stay away from it. A strategy that may make me tons of money in a hot market could very well tank when the market turns.

What sets the Strait Path system apart from almost every other form of real estate investing is one key word: *sustainability*. Strategies and systems that focus on profit alone may make money in the short-term, but they are unsustainable. This applies to *every* system that does not consider each of the six key elements equally and holistically. These inconsistent, unreliable forms of real estate include the following: rentals; fix-and-flip; lease options; speculative building; equity leveraging; distress sales, including short sales and foreclosures; land development, residential development, and commercial development; and multi-unit investing.

The Strait Path system is the most sustainable form of real estate investing available to most investors. It was created by studying all forms of real estate investing, identifying and incorporating the good elements of each, eliminating the flaws, and then putting it all together in a simple, streamlined, coherent, replicable, predictable, and safe system. It's the system I continue to apply with unwavering dedication in any market. It allows me to serve individuals, families, and society in ways that are impossible to accomplish with other systems. It always makes sense, everyone who applies it properly can be successful, and it avoids every pitfall that drags down investors who take the "broad and crooked paths."

Let's consider each of these six elements in turn to understand why they are so important. Each element is followed by questions to ask yourself as you're considering any type of investment. We will then compare and contrast the Strait Path system with other forms of real estate.

TIME

"Time is more valuable than money. You can get more money, but you cannot get more time."—Jim Rohn, author, *7 Strategies for Wealth and Happiness*

Real estate is a complex, multifaceted industry. From finding deals and negotiating to signing contracts and managing properties, it requires massive amounts of knowledge and time. However, not all systems are created equal. Each form of real estate has specific, intrinsic time commitments.

Never, ever underestimate the value of time. This is one of the biggest mistakes I see would-be investors make. People get excited about the prospects of real estate investing, jump in headfirst, and then spend way too much time doing the wrong things, or doing things that they shouldn't be doing themselves. The inability to delegate, and thus maximize, time is the curse of the do-it-yourself types.

Successful and sustainable real estate investing requires that you learn how to reduce the time you expend, while at the same time increasing your profits. The more time you spend on any individual deal, the less time you have to spend on creating multiple deals. The more time your strategy requires, the less successful you'll be, and you'll be inclined to wash out of real estate investing entirely. The more time an investment takes, the more it feels like a job, as opposed to a true investment, which should demand passive participation on your part.

The success of the Strait Path system is largely a function of speed. Speed is achieved by eliminating flawed perspectives and habits, focusing on the right deals in the right ways, and leveraging the time, talents, and efforts of others. In short, you've got to use the right system executed by the right people in the right ways.

> **Investment Analysis Questions**
>
> - How much time will this investment require?
> - Are there ways that I can reduce the amount of time I spend on each deal?
> - How can I leverage the time, talents, and efforts of other people while still managing the investment responsibly?

EFFORT

A strong work ethic can be both a virtue and a weakness. I've known many people who are proud that they are "hard workers," yet oftentimes working hard gets in the way of working smart. These hard workers often burn out when results don't meet expectations.

Does your real estate strategy require hard work, or smart work? Are you engaged in actual *productivity*, or mere *activity*? Just because a person exerts energy doesn't mean that he or she is producing real value. If that were true, you could shovel holes in your backyard and become a millionaire just through the activity of shoveling.

Productivity results in greater value. In other words, it results in profit in one form or another. Many real estate strategies require the exertion of energy that is often wasted. For example, a lot of fix-and-flip practitioners don't realize the difference between market value and perceived value. They put a lot of money, time, and effort into cosmetic fixes that don't raise the true market value of a home. Strait Path real estate, on the other hand, captures the market value without wasting all that energy.

I once met a man who had purchased fourteen investment properties in a city three hours from his home. After a year of six-hour commutes, he got burned out and sold the properties, even though he was making money. He learned the lesson that profit isn't the only consideration when it comes to investing.

> **Investment Analysis Questions**
> - How much effort and hands-on involvement will this investment require?
> - How can I reduce my effort?
> - Are the returns worth the effort?
> - Is this sustainable—can I keep putting forth this much energy for a long period of time, or will I burn out?

RISK

"The innovators I know are successful to the extent to which they define risks and confine them."—Peter Drucker, author, *Innovation and Entrepreneurship*

You've heard the cliché that if you want to increase your returns, you must increase your risk, right? Do you believe it? Do you think that commercial real estate investing is risky for Donald Trump? Do you think that building a business is risky for John Assaraf or Michael Gerber? Do you really believe that you have to choose between a conservative approach with low returns and a risky approach with high returns?

~~Typical Investing: High Risk = High Return~~
Strait Path Investing: Least Risk = High Return

That cliché is a deception perpetuated by institutions and individuals with vested interests—by convincing you to take on more risk, they can transfer their risk to you. High-risk investing isn't investing at all—it's gambling. It's for those who get a thrill from the game or for those who didn't work hard to earn their money (easy come, easy go). It's certainly possible to win big with high-risk investments, but it's more likely that you'll lose big.

Is this really how you want to live your life? Would you prefer to feel anxious or secure about your investment choices? When investing is done right, it's both safe and lucrative. It does require you to have more control and to be more actively involved than traditional investing, but it's doable. Our clients prove it every day.

REIC Investors Share Their Experience: John and Diane

"One of the fantastic benefits of the Strait Path system is the mitigated risk. With one of our investment properties, the buyer-tenants we had were unable to continue with the purchase of the home. The down payment they had made toward the house was enough for us to cover just a couple of mortgage payments, if it came to that. Luckily, we were able to find new tenants within the month, so we only had to cover one mortgage payment with that reserve down payment. The new buyer-tenants were able to invest even more to build immediate equity. They have been fantastic and are making improvements to the home while working toward ownership. They are planning to attend classes to prepare them for successful home ownership. This system really reduces risk for everyone—including tenants."

Personally, I'm highly averse to risk. I strive to do everything in my power to reduce risk and create certainty. I want to feel confident in my ability to earn a profit with each investment. This is why I reject 401(k)s, IRAs, and other similar vehicles—they're way too risky and I have far too little control over them. It's also why I shun any form of speculative real estate investing. I've analyzed every other form of real estate to be able to do just that. High-flying, risky strategies have no place on the Strait Path. No amount of money is worth the fear, anxiety, and uncertainty. And, interestingly enough, our system makes higher and more consistent returns than any other, while reducing the risk. This may sound paradoxical, given how often we're taught that high risk equals high returns. Once you understand Strait Path real estate, however, it becomes common sense.

Investment Analysis Questions

- How risky is this investment?
- What's the likelihood of its success/failure?
- What guarantees does this investment carry?
- Is this investment collateralized?
- Do I have a solid exit strategy?
- What options do I have if things go wrong?
- How can I reduce my risk as much as possible?

# SERVICE TO INDIVIDUALS AND SOCIETY

"If you help enough people get what they want, you will get what you want."—Zig Ziglar, author, *See You at the Top*

Every investment system that creates win-lose transactions and elevates investors at the expense of buyers will inevitably fail. Get-rich-quick schemes built on manipulation and deception are the fastest route to failure, the loss of self-respect, and destruction. The only sustainable, legitimate, and worthy path to wealth is to create real value for others—in other words, to serve people on their terms.

If you think that the only way to create wealth in real estate is to take advantage of the ignorance, fear, and/or greed of others, you're reading the wrong book. If your intention is solely to make as much money as possible for yourself, you will end up earning only a fraction of what is possible if you were to focus more on helping others.

Service to others is a key to wealth creation. Those who serve the most earn the most. Exploiters may enjoy wealth, but they don't enjoy peace of mind and self-respect, and their wealth is almost always short-lived.

Investment Analysis Questions

- How well does this system/strategy serve others?
- How could it better serve others?
- Is this system fair and equitable?
- Does it create win/lose scenarios in any form and to any degree?
- Does it take advantage of fear, greed, and/or desperation?
- Will it put everyone else involved in the transaction in a better, or a worse, situation?

MARKET VOLATILITY

Anyone who thinks that it's impossible to make money through real estate in a diving or stagnant market is using the wrong system. Why would anyone want to spend time, money, and effort building something that will eventually crumble because of market forces beyond their control? Why would anyone want to be subject to the whims of the market?

Of course, nobody wants insecurity and instability, but most people don't know how to *create* security and stability with their investments. They follow the mainstream financial media, which teaches that "diversification" and "dollar cost averaging" are the keys to financial security. The implicit message is that you can do nothing to control your investments: since you are subject to the fickleness of the market, the only route to take is to invest in a lot of different things, and then hope and pray that everything doesn't plummet at the same time.

"Wide diversification is only required when investors do not understand what they are doing."—Warren Buffett, investor, philanthropist

---

The truth is that long-term financial stability *can* be created. It is possible to secure almost full immunity from market fluctuations. In fact, the Strait Path system doesn't even depend on appreciation to be profitable; what the market does is practically irrelevant. In contrast, most real estate strategies require market cooperation. Strait Path followers view appreciation as icing on the cake—it's nice to have, but it's not necessary to enjoy sweet deals. They know that depending on appreciation is speculative investing—in other words, gambling. Market appreciation is beyond the control of the individual investor. We teach investors to profit from the things they can control. If things go well beyond that sphere, they benefit, and when things turn sour, they're protected.

Investment Analysis Questions

- Will this system/strategy work in every market?
- Can I earn a profit when the market is going up *and* when the market is going down?
- How protected am I from market volatility?
- How far does the market have to drop before I am adversely affected?
- Do I have a long-term strategy to profit if the market does drop so low that it hurts me?
- How big is the market for this investment? Is it a broad, or a niche market?
- What percentage of people will be able to afford this investment?

PROFITABILITY

"It's not how much money you make, but how much you keep, how hard it works for you, and how many generations you keep it for."—Robert Kiyosaki, author, *Who Took My Money?*

For most investors, profitability is the primary, and in some cases sole, factor used to decide whether or not to invest in something. They fly from deal to deal with no system in place. Like an eager puppy that runs to whoever will pet it, they rush into any deal as long as they're convinced that it will make them money. Unfortunately for them, their profits are as fleeting as their focus. They make good money on one deal, average money on another, and lose money on the next. They're reduced to calculating returns based on averages over time, rather than the performance of each individual deal.

Also, investors who elevate profit above all other factors are those who tend to spend money as fast as they make it. They have to keep making it in order to support their extravagant lifestyle, which creates a self-reinforcing cycle. They become addicted to money and lose the ability to put it in its proper perspective as a tool and a byproduct, rather than an end in itself.

In Strait Path real estate, we're not just looking to make money—we seek sustainable, consistent, and predictable profits. We don't want the *highest* returns—we want the *best* returns when considered in light of every other investment factor. Without a holistic approach, perspectives on profit become misguided. No amount of money is worth exposure to high risk and/or creating a win-lose transaction. The more time and effort you have to spend on a deal, the less it should be worth to you. The more you must depend on appreciation, the less appealing the opportunity becomes.

The Five Profit Centers on the Strait Path

The interesting thing about Strait Path real estate is that even though profitability is one of *six* factors considered for every deal, the Strait Path system is still far more profitable than other forms of investing. In other words, the Strait Path system is still the best even when profitability is an investor's sole or primary focus.

This is because the system offers five profit centers, whereas others offer only one or two. The five profit centers include 1) discount equity, 2) cash flow, 3) down payment, 4) appreciation, and 5) tax benefits.

1. Discount Equity Discount equity is the difference between the market value and the purchase price of a home. Our finding system helps us secure properties with 15 percent equity or more. Depending upon the size of the home and its discount purchase price, you may make more on one purchase than you make all year in your current job. For example, if a home is worth $275,000 and you can purchase it at a 15 percent discount for $233,750, you'll make $41,250 on the purchase alone.

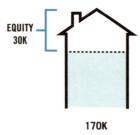

2. Cash Flow Cash flow is the monthly amount you receive from your tenants less your monthly mortgage payment. In short, it's the difference between your mortgage payment and what your tenant pays you each month.

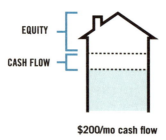

3. Down Payment The technical term for this is "option consideration," which is a fee paid by tenants to secure their opportunity to purchase the home within a specified period of time. This is nonrefundable, and we receive on average $5,000 down per house.

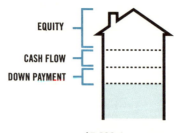

4. Appreciation Appreciation is the rise in value of a property over time due to increased demand. What's notable about Strait Path real estate is that we don't rely on appreciation to turn a profit, though we do account for it when it occurs.

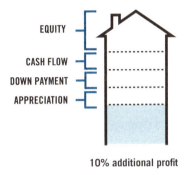

10% additional profit

5. Tax Benefits Tax law allows homeowners to deduct mortgage interest from their taxes. This is a huge advantage in Strait Path real estate, since the goal is to purchase as many homes as possible.

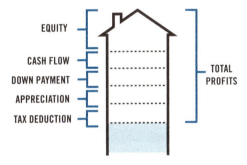

With a fixer-upper, investors receive the first profit center and, if they're lucky, the fourth. But they have no cash flow, they do not get a down payment, and capital gains taxes often wipe out any earnings. With rentals, investors enjoy tax benefits and sometimes benefit from property appreciation. They receive no down payment, however, and they're lucky if they get a good deal up front and receive a positive cash flow. Once again, the Strait Path system offers investors all five income streams.

> **Investment Analysis Questions**
>
> - How much profit can I create from this investment?
>
> - Am I benefiting from as many profit centers as possible, or am I missing out on other potential sources of profitability?
>
> - Is the profit worth the amount of time, effort, and risk involved?
>
> - How certain is my profit from this deal, even if the market drops?
>
> - Am I deriving profit in an ethical manner?
>
> - Do I have a system in place to create sustainable, consistent, and predictable profits, or is this a one-time strategy?

COMPETING FORMS OF REAL ESTATE INVESTING: THE GOOD, THE BAD, AND THE UGLY

There are obviously countless types and variations of real estate investing. When I created the Strait Path system, I studied every system and strategy I could find, all of which fall in the general categories of 1) rentals, 2) fix-and-flip, 3) lease options, 4) distress sales, including short sales and foreclosures, 5) multi-unit investing, 6) speculative building, and 7) land development, residential development, and commercial development.

I wanted a system that was simple, safe, replicable, and predictable, and that could be applied without needing massive amounts of time, knowledge, experience, and capital. I wanted to create something that anyone, regardless of his or her current circumstances, could apply successfully without taking on a lot of risk. I therefore eliminated the last three general categories, though I considered them in depth. Multi-unit investing, spec building, and new development are simply not available to most investors. For our purposes, we'll compare Strait Path real estate to only the first four categories.

Let's consider each of these in turn to ascertain the strong points and drawbacks of each.

Rentals

Rentals are the most common form of real estate for average investors. The concept is simple and straightforward and doesn't require a lot of sophistication: you purchase a property, and then rent it out and hope that you can earn a positive cash flow.

The Good

- Rentals create a monthly cash flow (though many rental owners experience negative cash flow).

- Rentals are usually in demand, depending on the type and size of the home.

- The buy-and-hold strategy means that appreciation and long-term profitability are almost guaranteed—as long as the investor holds onto the property long enough.

- Investors enjoy tax savings by writing off mortgage interest payments.

The Bad

- Investors expend significant time and effort fulfilling landlord duties.

- ▶ On paper a rental seems to be a good holding strategy, but most people sell rentals in a few short years—often at a loss—because they get so fed up with them.

- ▶ It's very difficult to get a positive cash flow from rentals in the first few years.

- ▶ High occupancy turnover means that investors have to get new tenants frequently.

The Ugly

- ▶ It's relatively common for renters to damage the home, in some cases significantly.

- ▶ The investor is responsible for all repairs, resulting in high out-of-pocket expenses. The investor must paint the inside of the home and replace the carpet periodically. He or she must pay for broken furnaces, air conditioners, garage doors, appliances, etc.

- ▶ The investor is on call twenty-four hours a day, seven days a week, unless he hires a property management company, but doing so substantially reduces profits.

- ▶ Some rentals are located in undesirable neighborhoods, which can increase risk.

- ▶ Rentals return significantly less revenue than properties acquired using the Strait Path system, as shown in the tables on page 66 and 67.

Fix-and-Flip

Fix-and-flip is another popular, though unsustainable, strategy. The idea is to identify a home in need of repairs, buy it at a discount, fix it up, and then sell it for a profit. But flipping requires so much time and effort and is subject to so much risk that almost everyone who tries it gets burned, burned out, or both—even if they actually enjoy home improvement work.

I know an individual who has done twenty-one fixer-uppers over the course of about twenty years. He chose this strategy because he loves working with his hands and the process of beautifying homes. Even though almost all of his deals were profitable, he's stopped doing them and has taken a corporate job instead. He realized that it just wasn't working—he was never going to achieve lasting wealth by doing it. He's a particularly poignant example because I don't know of anyone better than he is at fixing and flipping homes. He, like so many others, realized that flipping was an unsustainable strategy.

I met another man who made a $10,000 profit on a flip. But after he did the math, he realized that he had earned the equivalent of $12 an hour.

The only time I've ever lost money in a real estate deal was on my fourth investment, which I purchased to flip. I bought it for $300,000, and I had solid comparables to substantiate a $400,000 market value. I was so excited by that amount of supposed equity that I jumped on the deal. After being on the market for ninety days, the home eventually sold at a $5,000 loss to me. I assumed it would act like a typical flip, but it was way over the median home price for the area. The lessons I learned were 1) avoid houses above the median price, and 2) flipping is unreliable. It may work consistently for some people, but it requires so much intricate knowledge and experience that newbies are virtually guaranteed to lose on the strategy.

The Profitability of the Strait Path System vs. Renting

Assumptions
Size: 5 bed/2 bath
Value: $235,000
Purchase price: $200,000
Down payment: $40,000
Loan amount: $160,000
Interest rate: 6.5%
Payment (Principal, Interest, Taxes, Insurance, or PITI): $1,150

The Profitability of the Strait Path System vs. Renting			
Compassionate Financing		**Renting**	
Income		Income	
Down payment	$5,000 ($208/mo)	Deposit	$500
Rent	$1,300/mo	Rent	$1,150/mo
Cash flow	$358/mo	Cash flow	$0/mo
Expenses		Expenses	
Repairs	$0/mo	Repairs	$75/mo
Management	$0/mo	Management	$104/mo (9% of rental income)
Total leasing benefit over five years	$21,480	Total renting benefit over five years	-$10,740

Selling Home After Five Years of Holding			
Compassionate Financing		**Renting**	
Sales price	$265,000	Sales price	$265,000
Repair costs	$0	Repair costs	$15,000
Discount	$0	Discount	$20,000 (7.5% of market value)
Agent fees	$0	Agent fees	$14,700
Tenant benefit	$10,000	Tenant benefit	$0
Total sales benefit	$55,000	Total sales benefit	$15,300

Total Profits			
Compassionate Financing		**Renting**	
Total leasing benefit	$21,480	Total renting benefit	–$10,740
Total sales benefit	$55,000	Total sales benefit	$15,300
Total profit	$76,480	Total profit	$4,560

*Rent increases not factored in
*Closing cost on the sale not factored in
*Sales price growth between 2–3%

The Good

▶ When done right, fixer-uppers are bought at substantial discounts. Securing up-front equity is an excellent way to mitigate risk.

The Bad

▶ The difference between market value and perceived value often dictates that relatively little of your time, money, and effort will result in increased actual value (see chapter 6).

▶ Lending requirements make it extremely difficult to get an accurate appraisal within a few months of purchasing a home. You may buy a home for $150,000 and then put $40,000 into it in the hopes of getting an appraisal for $230,000. But an $80,000 jump in value within a few months is a huge red flag for banks, so appraisers are less willing to account for it, which makes flip homes more difficult to sell quickly.

▶ Flipping creates a full-time job, rather than passive income. You have to keep doing it over and over again or else the cash flow stops. This is a major drawback even for those who love to do it.

The Ugly

- ▶ Most people don't consider every variable, which means that their calculations are wrong. It may appear that a home has $40,000 of equity, but that number can be whittled down quickly to nothing after factoring in capital gains taxes, realtor fees, monthly payments, fix-up costs, and the inevitable devaluation of the property to sell it fast. Initial excitement can often very quickly turn into a nightmare scenario where you're lucky to break even, or where you actually lose money.

- ▶ Most flips must be purchased with 40 to 50 percent equity for them to be profitable. These deals are nearly impossible to find, especially for beginners.

- ▶ All things considered, the most successful flippers find that the return on their time and money equals that of a decent-paying job. In other words, they would be better off to work a little overtime at their current job, rather than falling into the flipping trap.

- ▶ Flip deals carry a high risk of market dependency. The entire strategy is predicated on re-selling the home quickly. Therefore, if the market drops while you're fixing up a home, all your equity goes down the drain. Without a hold strategy, you have no way of earning it back—you're forced to liquidate the home as quickly as possible. You'll feel lucky to break even, and in many cases you'll lose money.

Lease Options

A lease option is exactly what it sounds like: as tenants lease a home for a monthly amount, they secure the option to purchase the home under the terms of an agreement. Lease options are gateways to home ownership for renters.

The Good

- ▶ Like rentals, lease options create a monthly cash flow. Moreover, the cash flow is generally at least $200 per month higher than what is garnered with comparable rentals because lessees are willing to pay more for the benefits they're receiving.

- ▶ The higher monthly lease payments improve the investor's debt-to-income ratios, thus increasing his or her ability to finance more homes. With rentals, an investor's credit is often maxed out after acquiring just a few properties.

- ▶ Investors can collect a nonrefundable down payment from lessees.

- ▶ There is no property maintenance for the investor. In lease options, the tenant assumes all responsibility for repairs and improvements.

- ▶ Tax savings. Investors can deduct mortgage interest from their income taxes because they own the home.

- ▶ The investor saves 6 percent on realtor fees when the home sells.

- ▶ For tenants, lease options can be an excellent way to achieve home ownership, which is otherwise unavailable to them. Tenants love having a place they can call home, being able to make home improvements, and not throwing away rent money. Also, tenants can get into homes with a relatively small amount of money needed for a down payment.

▶ Lease options buy time for tenants to repair their credit and prepare for traditional financing.

▶ Tenants can walk away from the home with no liability.

▶ The transaction doesn't show up on the buyer's credit.

The Bad

▶ Traditional lease-option contracts create an inevitable win-lose scenario on the back-end sale by setting a purchase price up front. If the property appreciates, the investor loses; if the property depreciates, the tenant loses.

▶ Lease options have a high failure rate, meaning that most tenants will not be able to secure traditional financing by the end of the term.

The Ugly

▶ Many investors use lease options to prey on unsuspecting, naïve homebuyers. They collect a large down payment, and then, when the tenants are unable to purchase the home, they get rid of them and bring in new suckers. They cycle tenants through to collect hefty down payments.

Distress Sales

Distress sales include short sales, foreclosures, auctions, divorce sales, etc. Scouring the landscape for distress sales—or what I call "ambulance chasing"—is a common tactic. The idea is to find people in bad and/or urgent situations who need to sell quickly. Whatever the reason, these sellers are willing to sell their homes at far below market value.

I'm referring here to a specific way of finding properties, rather than a complete strategy for investing. I've included it because it can be employed in all forms of real estate, but it must be understood that Strait Path real estate rejects the negative aspects of searching for distress sales.

The Good

- ▶ These homes can be purchased at substantial discounts, thus decreasing the investor's risk.

- ▶ When done properly (and contrary to popular thinking), this actually performs a valuable service for people who feel lucky to be rid of the burden. In many cases, they would have lost the home to foreclosure anyway, so it saves them from damaging their credit for years.

The Bad

- ▶ Successfully dealing with short sales and foreclosures in particular requires a high degree of specialized knowledge. This knowledge is certainly available, but few know how to find it, or have the discipline needed to follow through.

▶ Fierce competition among investors clamoring for the same properties makes these properties much more difficult to obtain.

▶ It generally takes a lot of time and effort to identify the right properties, especially since many of them are "for sale by owner"; finding these "nonlistings" requires a lot of driving and legwork.

▶ Since the primary focus is on the initial purchase, the back-end liquidation strategy is often neglected.

▶ Distressed properties become increasingly difficult to find in boom markets. In other words, the strategy is market dependent.

The Ugly

▶ This type of investing can degenerate and become predatory when done by the wrong people, and in the wrong ways.

After reviewing these common forms of real estate, imagine a system that embodies the best of all systems and strategies and eliminates the pitfalls and flaws. Imagine a low-risk system requiring a minimal time and effort commitment, and that works in any market, serves individuals and communities at high levels, and creates higher, more sustainable, and more diverse profits than any other. Imagine a system that gives you the cash flow of rentals and lease options, without the hassle of property management and the dangers of exploitation. Imagine a system that enjoys the discounts and appreciation of flipping, but without the risk. This is Strait Path real estate.

	Rentals	Fix-and-Flips	Lease Options	Strait Path
Time	Part-time job	Excessive	Minimal	**Minimal**
Effort	Part-time job	Excessive	Minimal	**Minimal**
Risk	Minimal	High	Medium	**None**
Service	Moderate	Low	Medium (potential to be harmful)	**Maximum**
Market volatility	Minimal risk	High risk; best in hot markets	Moderate risk; best in recovering markets	**Any market**
Profitability	Minimal in the short-term	Volatile	Moderate	**Maximum**
(Profit centers)	Discount equity; cash flow; down payment; appreciation	Discount equity; cash flow	Down payment; appreciation; tax benefits	**Discount equity; cash flow; down payment; appreciation; tax benefits**

I'll conclude this chapter by sharing the story of one of our club members, in his own words:

REIC Investor Rob Shares His Experience

"I have been investing—and helping others invest—in real estate since 2003. And since 2006, for better or for worse, it has been my full-time profession. Through much success and much failure, I believe I now have enough experience in this game to speak with authority. In a relatively short period of time, I have experienced, in one degree or another, most of the investing spectrum. As a result, I have formed beliefs about how someone should (and should not) invest their hard-earned dollars.

"Anyone can go to Barnes & Noble, pick up any book in the investing section, and learn about great ways to make a lot of money in real estate. And there are a lot more than thirty-one flavors to choose from. I've also learned that if that person were to precisely follow most of the programs in those books, handsome returns would most likely follow. There is also no shortage of seminars, videos, and audio books that a person can pay shocking amounts of money for, which will work. I believe I have heard of, and probably tried, just about all of the flavors.

"So what advice would I give to someone starting with little or no experience? I would say simply this: The fact is that there are good deals in real estate and there are fantastic deals in real estate. The trick is to be able to distinguish between the two, ignore the good, and focus your efforts on the fantastic.

"To make a long story short, Strait Path real estate is not too good to be true; it is simply very, very good. In fact, it is fantastic. If I can give you one word of advice while you are considering whether this is the real deal or not, it would be this: Get over it and get to work. You *will* lose sleep as the reality of how fantastic this opportunity is sinks in. You *will* direct conversations with your friends and family to talking about this. You *will* make money. A lot of money. I believe this is the opportunity of my lifetime."

So far you've been introduced to how and why Strait Path real estate was created. You've learned that it requires a specific mind-set, or worldview, as contrasted with the traditional "401(k) mind-set." You've learned that it's intended for *everyone* as a replacement to outdated and severely flawed retirement strategies and products. You've been given a brief overview of the system so that the details of each individual part will make sense within the bigger context. You've learned the six key elements of successful investing and why these make the Strait Path superior to any other real estate system.

With this foundation in place, now you'll explore each phase of the system in greater detail. You'll learn how to create a portfolio game plan and how this helps you stay on the path. You'll identify assets that may be hidden from you now, assets that you can leverage immediately to your benefit. You'll be given the secrets of how we consistently find properties at 15 percent discounts or greater. You'll learn how important it is to finance your properties the right way to purchase as many as possible. Finally, you'll be exposed to the heart and soul of the Strait Path system: Compassionate Financing. You'll learn how this serves people and why service matters. You'll learn how to structure contracts to provide the greatest protection, both for you and for your tenants. You'll learn how to maximize your returns through five profit centers.

So let's start with creating your portfolio game plan.

Creating Your Portfolio Game Plan

"To begin with the end in mind means to start with a clear understanding of your destination. It means to know where you are going so that you better understand where you are now and so that the steps you take are always in the right direction."

—Stephen R. Covey

No wealth creation system would be complete without a vision of the end goal. A game plan provides motivation when things are tough and discipline to turn away from temptation. For example, a person who invests in real estate without a clear plan but with the hope of making money may do well on her first property and then be tempted to use the profits to buy a boat. Her standard of living may rise slightly by doing so, but her long-term financial security will actually decrease. To be successful, you need a structured and systematized approach to investing. This is achieved by constructing a portfolio game plan.

A solid portfolio game plan in the Strait Path system requires the following elements:

- ▶ Identifying and leveraging hidden assets
- ▶ A ten-year, customized goal
- ▶ Enduring to the end

IDENTIFYING AND LEVERAGING HIDDEN ASSETS

Russell Conwell, a minister and the founder of Temple University, once gave a lecture titled "Acres of Diamonds." He related the story of an Arab man who wanted to become rich. Informed by an old priest that he would find diamonds in "a river that runs through white sands, between high mountains," the man sold his farm and set off on his quest to find diamonds. Years later, having found no diamonds, his money spent, and his spirit defeated, he drowned himself in the sea. Soon after, the man to whom he had sold his farm found "the most magnificent diamond mine in all the history of mankind."

Investing for most Americans is similar. We want money so badly that we search high and low for people, resources, knowledge, strategies, and schemes. More often than not, we get burned. What few people realize is how many assets are readily available to them. These assets are hidden because of how we've been trained through media and culture.

Successful investors understand how to shift, position, and leverage assets that are hidden from or are underutilized by most individuals. They realize that economic success comes from producing higher yields from existing resources. As the economist Jean-Baptiste Say wrote in *A Treatise on Political Economy*, "Creating wealth is a function of moving assets from areas of low yield to areas of high yield."

This sounds simple conceptually, but applying it practically requires a paradigm shift for most people. Why? Because their low-yield assets, including home equity and 401(k), IRA, and other qualified-plan money, are the "sacred cows" of traditional retirement planning. In the Strait Path system, we strongly recommend that our clients shift these low-yield assets to areas of high yield, namely real estate investing.

When I first met Dave, he had a lot of equity in his home but not a lot of expendable income. He had a goal to pay off his home, so we helped him put that goal on steroids. Using his home equity, we bought five investment properties, which have put him on track to create $500,000 in net profit in the next few years. He'll be able to pay off his home and still have more than $400,000 left to continue investing. These are the kinds of possibilities that open up when we shift assets from low-yield areas to areas of high yield.

401(k)s and IRAs are similar. In a thirty-year time frame, you're lucky to receive an 8 to 10 percent average rate of return. Doesn't 50 percent or more sound better—especially in light of the current economic downturn?

My friend and client Mark was able to liquidate and leverage his 401(k) successfully. When we were creating his portfolio game plan, we were torn between using his home equity or his 401(k). We decided to use his 401(k) because he was living month-to-month, and refinancing his mortgage would have increased the monthly payment by several hundred dollars. Even though we knew that his new investment cash flow would offset that payment increase, we wanted to make sure he would be safe. He liquidated his 401(k) and bought two investment properties that together generate $650 per month of positive cash flow. Furthermore, those properties will most likely yield him $225,000 net profit within four years.

"But what about taxes and penalties?" you may be thinking. My perspective is that this is just the cost of doing business, not to mention the lost opportunity costs that must be factored in. It simply comes down to doing the math. I don't hesitate to pay relatively minor penalties and taxes when I know I can generate much higher and safer returns through real estate. Understand that I am not being flippant about your hard-earned money. I don't take financial losses lightly; in fact, this is precisely why I teach people to liquidate home equity and qualified plans as quickly as possible. I just know that there is a far better system than the 30-plus-year "you're in it for the long haul" mind-set. Furthermore, there are ways to defer penalties and taxes on qualified accounts through real estate anyway.

This is a perfect example of why developing the investor mind-set is fundamental to the Strait Path system. It requires a recognition that traditional retirement advice is flawed and obsolete, a belief that there are better options, and the knowledge to apply those options safely and sustainably. I don't want you to increase your risk—I want to help you *decrease* your risk. I want you to pay off your home. I don't want you to put your hard-earned retirement funds in danger—I want you to maximize their returns. Wealth is created when we shift assets to increase their productivity. Home equity and qualified-plan funds are low-yield assets that can be leveraged to generate abundant wealth.

I urge you to think hard about the inherent risks of the traditional mind-set—your financial future depends on it. Even if you enjoy relative success with the traditional route, it's rarely enough to give you a secure and comfortable retirement. Those who pay off their house and have a little left in qualified plans are often eventually forced to sell their home or use a reverse mortgage to prolong their retirement. That's just one risk, and overwhelming risk is the reality of the traditional investment mind-set.

One of my clients, Lance, is a financial planner. Though he's bombarded daily with investment opportunities, he rejects most of them because he readily recognizes that they're not financially sound. He's naturally a skeptical person, but when he researched the Strait Path system he was astounded by how it revolutionizes the real estate industry. He was further amazed with the results of his first property. He was able to purchase and control it with $15,000, and he's now receiving a cash flow of $600 per month, which is unheard of with traditional investments. He projects that he'll make $95,000 within two years, which would be an annual return of 317 percent. After experiencing this success, Lance now discusses Strait Path real estate with all of his clients, and he's referred many of them to us. He's convinced that the system is a far better and safer opportunity than most traditional investment options.

Tangible assets, such as cash in 401(k)s, are relatively easy to identify. However, the two most common hidden assets are ==income and credit.== A solid work history and income combined with an average credit score can produce far more leverage and investment returns than most people realize. Anyone in such a situation can start with zero assets and end up with millions in a few short years, as I have done. A job and credit were all I started out with. The financial recipe to our ten-year game plan is one tablespoon of credit and one tablespoon of job, plus a cup of time and one cup of our system; then pop it in the oven of repetition, and end up with $2 million after baking your plan for ten years. That's a little corny, I know, but it really is that simple—and that's the conservative path.

My neighbor Duane is an optometrist. Having invested mostly in the stock market, he wanted to add real estate to his portfolio, especially after seeing me succeed. He approached me and we quickly found two properties for him. He has never set foot on the properties, yet today he earns $766 per month on them because of our partnership. He received down payments totaling $10,000 and enjoys $114,000 of combined equity.

My friend Scott is another perfect example of leveraging one's income and credit score. Scott was also highly invested in the stock market, as well as in his own companies. He had considered real estate in the past but had never acted on it. He partnered with our team and leveraged our experience, time, effort, and systems to buy a property in a neighboring city. Like Duane, he's never been to the property. Today he has $16,000 in his bank account from the transaction. He also has a positive cash flow of $739 per month and $80,000 of equity.

Yet another hidden asset is your ==relationships.== You can partner with family members, coworkers, business partners, and friends to purchase investment properties that would otherwise be inaccessible to you.

Creative partnering is the real secret of almost all real estate gurus. This is how they accomplish so much in such a short time. While I don't consider myself a "guru," my story is similar in that regard. I've done plenty of real estate deals on my own, but I've done far more through partnerships. My father-in-law was my first partner. After watching me succeed for a couple of years, he wanted to know what I was doing. I taught him the system, and he wanted to be involved. I provided the know-how and the work, and he offered his money, credit, and job history. Together, we have purchased thirty-one properties.

The system I teach in this book is precisely what I have done to succeed. It's not theory or salesmanship. It is the compounded result of hundreds of actual real estate deals, most of which were executed through partnerships.

I want to drive home this point to help you understand how powerful partnerships can be. Partnering is far more than something you should do if you don't have other options. I encourage every investor to actively seek sound partnerships from the very beginning. It's one of the best forms of leverage and an excellent way to propel you forward much faster than you could go alone. We'll discuss this in greater detail in chapter eight.

> **Strait Path Sign #1**
>
> Identify low-yield assets and leverage them by moving them to high-yield investments. Low-yield assets are often hidden, and may include home equity, qualified-plan funds, income, job history, credit history, relationships, and cash. This may require a paradigm shift. Achieve this and manage your risk through education.

One of the great things about the Strait Path system is that there are very few people who are *unable* to participate in it. Once hidden assets are understood and uncovered, it leaves people without an excuse to start investing. Once again, these assets include, but are not limited to, home equity; retirement-fund money in low-yield, risky accounts; income; work history; credit history; relationships; and cash. Everyone can participate, even those with very little assets to begin with. In their case, it's just a matter of time.

YOUR TEN-YEAR, CUSTOMIZED GOAL

Everyone I work with creates a ten-year goal along with a customized plan for achieving that goal. This plan includes both beginning and end goals. The beginning goal is to uncover and transfer enough existing assets to purchase one home (other people with more assets can begin by purchasing multiple homes). The end goal is to create enough cash and cash flow to be able to technically "retire" within ten years, which is a realistic goal for *every* individual. When financed and positioned properly, investment properties create a chain reaction; the more you have, the more you're able to leverage.

There are four specific paths to achieve wealth through the Strait Path system, all of which coincide with four general situations. The main difference between them is the speed at which people can become wealthy through investing in real estate. The first path can be compared to walking, the second to riding a bike, the third to driving a car, and the fourth to flying a plane, all of which end at the same destination. These paths are outlined below. Notice that each new path requires fewer steps than the preceding path. Becoming familiar with these paths will help you create your ten-year game plan.

Path #1: Preparing for the Journey

The person on path #1 has bad credit, no credit, or not enough credit to secure traditional financing, and either doesn't have a job or hasn't established a two-year work history within one industry. People who have filed bankruptcy and young adults often fit this category.

I personally had to wait fourteen months from the time I knew I wanted to invest in real estate to when I was able to buy my first home. At that time I lacked two years of work history, so I consciously worked toward it.

Steps on the Path

For people on path #1, the primary goal is to become qualified for traditional financing. The path is as follows:

1. Establish a healthy credit score that can be leveraged to purchase real estate.

2. Establish a two-year work history within one industry.

3. Save money for down payments.

4. While working on loan qualification, you can implement creative real estate to begin investing immediately. This can be done either through sandwich financing or partnerships. To help you do this, we've created a free download called "How to Execute Creative Real Estate Investing," which you'll find at www.straitpathrealestate.com.

5. Upon qualifying for traditional financing and building a property portfolio, keep leveraging your credit, income, and assets to buy more properties. Understand that with Strait Path investing, each house will sell within one to five years. Before a house sells, we can refinance it to pull out equity, which is then used to purchase another home. Through refinances and selling homes your portfolio expands, and your profits experience exponential growth.

Justin, one of our investors, has enjoyed tremendous success on this path. At twenty-one years old, Justin had no credit, no capital, no experience with real estate investing, and no intentions of doing it. He was studying business at a local college. After accepting a position as a personal research assistant within our firm, he learned all about the system and grew excited about its possibilities.

Justin's parents were a perfect fit for the system, so he began teaching them with the hope of partnering with them. Not only were they extremely skeptical, they also had no time for real estate investing. His father owns a public relations firm and his mother is a full-time CPA. Fortunately, he was able to convince them to attend a seminar. They were both surprised and impressed that they could find no holes in the system. After researching Strait Path thoroughly, they signed up for the program and Justin had his partnership—he with time but no capital, and his parents with no time and a lot of capital. Using his parents' money and credit, Justin did all the legwork to secure two investment properties and find tenants for them. Their first home was purchased at a 21 percent discount with $64,000 of equity. They received $7,000 down from their tenant, and it cash flows $50 per month. The second home was purchased at a 27 percent discount with $80,000 of equity. They received $3,000 down, and it cash flows $300 per month.

Now twenty-three, Justin continues to improve his ability to invest personally. While currently focusing on sandwich financing deals, he is also establishing a work and credit history. When he and his parents sell their two homes and cash out, he can take his portion of the earnings and use it as capital on his own investments.

The Key to Path #1
Preparation is the key to this first path. The better qualified an individual is for traditional financing, the more properties he or she can buy, and thus the faster he or she can build momentum and wealth.

Path #2: Heading Toward the On-Ramp

The person on path #2 has good credit and an established job and work history, but has no other tangible assets to speak of, including a home. Young renters are often found in this category.

Steps on the Path

For people on path #2, the primary goal is to purchase either a personal residence or an investment property. Their path is the following:

1. Save enough money for a down payment.

2. Buy a home, either to live in or as an immediate investment. In either case, the purchase should be a discounted property.

3. As soon as possible, refinance or get a home equity line of credit (HELOC) on the first property, and use the cash to buy another property.

4. Keep repeating this process to build a large portfolio.

Ben is one of our investors who started on path #2 at the age of twenty-five. After graduating from college, he had a decent job and good credit, but he was renting and had no other real assets. After he learned our system, he realized that his credit and job history were hidden assets that could be wisely leveraged. While his peers and colleagues were all stuck in the renting trap, he had gained an entirely new perspective and was thinking in ways he hadn't before.

He saved up some money, and then found and purchased an excellent home with a mother-in-law apartment. With a sales price of $170,000 and a market value of $220,000, the property had a 23 percent equity position. Since Ben was single, he rented out the mother-in-law apartment, as well as three rooms in the home, collecting a total of $1,500 per month. His mortgage was $1,550 per month, so he was essentially living for free in a home that had increased his net worth by $50,000. Furthermore, since purchasing the home he has made improvements, and it has been rezoned into a duplex, which has increased the property's value to about $230,000.

About six months after the rezoning, Ben got married, and he and his wife wanted their own home. They secured a home equity line of credit on their first home, which they then put down on a second home. With a purchase price of $230,000 and a market value of $280,000, this bumped Ben's net worth up another $50,000. This home also has a mother-in-law apartment, which he and his wife rent out for $750 per month.

Ben and his wife later refinanced the mortgage on their first property. They recently secured a tenant for that home, receiving $3,000 down and $1,500 per month for a positive monthly cash flow of $500. Ben is now twenty-eight years old, he and his wife have a child, and they are ecstatic about how much they've been able to accomplish at such a young age. They are working on buying their third investment, which will hopefully close this year.

To put this in context, when Ben first started on the Strait Path he was earning $13 per hour at his "day" job. At that rate, the $1,250 he earns monthly from his two properties is the equivalent of working an additional ninety-six hours of work per month, or twenty-four more hours per week. And keep in mind that his investment income is passive.

The Key to Path #2

Purchasing their first discounted property is the key for individuals on this path, with the ultimate goal of leveraging their equity into more properties.

Path #3: Accelerating

The person on path #3 has an established credit and job history, solid income, and a home with equity.

Steps on the Path

1. Extract home equity through a refinance or HELOC, and then purchase a first investment property at a discount.

2. As soon as possible, do the same thing with the investment property—extract and leverage the equity into another investment.

3. Repeat the process to build a larger portfolio.

Amanda and Aaron, a couple in the REIC program, have recently started on this path. Amanda is a highly successful and popular radio personality, author, and speaker, and Aaron is a stay-at-home father. Amanda was realizing that, despite her great income, she would never be able to provide for her family like she wanted through her labor alone. She knew she needed to find dependable sources of passive income in order to leverage herself. In fact, she had been looking for opportunities for a couple of years prior to meeting me.

After I first met with Amanda and Aaron, they read through and discussed our materials and manuals. After another personal meeting, they were ready to move forward. They appreciated how commonsensical our system is and how simple it is for anyone to follow. They loved how it helped people who were unable to get approved for traditional financing. The concept of identifying and leveraging hidden assets resonated with them. In their case, this included their income, credit scores, and home equity. Furthermore, they recognized how their portfolio could grow exponentially as they stuck with the system over time. As I mapped out their ten-year portfolio game plan, they began to feel excited about the possibilities.

Our first step was to refinance their home to extract $45,000 of equity, which still left them 20 percent home equity in order to avoid paying mortgage insurance. The equity was used to purchase their first investment home. With an 18 percent equity position, the home immediately increased their net worth by $47,000. They received a $7,000 option consideration up front, along with the first three months of rent. Their monthly positive cash flow is $520.

They're now poised and looking forward to repeating this process over time. When their tenants purchase this first investment home, they will use the cash to purchase at least two more homes, probably within two years.

The Key to Path #3

Leveraging existing equity is the key to this path. Home equity is a hidden, dead asset unless it is put to use. Even if a person's goal is to pay off his or her home (which I recommend), he or she can achieve this goal more quickly by purchasing more real estate.

Path #4: Cruising Speed

The person on path #4 has a high credit score, great income and job history, a personal residence with equity, and other assets, including, but not limited to, a 401(k), IRAs, annuities, permanent life insurance policies, mutual funds and other liquid investments, or a business.

Steps on the Path

1. Leverage all equity and assets to purchase as many investment homes as possible.

2. Repeat the process to build a larger portfolio.

Matt, my father-in-law whom I mentioned earlier, is a textbook case of this fourth path. A part owner and salesman for a highly successful consulting firm, he had accumulated almost a million dollars, which was diversified among money market accounts, mutual funds, a 401(k), and IRAs. These funds did nothing but stagnate over the course of about ten years, so he began thinking of ways to manage that money better. Although he had had a number of negative experiences with real estate in the past, after seeing my system succeed and learning more about what I was doing, he started coming around to the idea of investing in real estate.

After buying a number of homes, I was looking for partners so I could continue leveraging. I approached him with one particular deal, the timing was right, and he partnered with me and paid cash for the home.

Later, we refinanced the home to roll the cash into another home, and then kept repeating the process. Since then, and over the course of about three years, we have bought thirty-one homes together, and we still own twenty-seven of those today. Matt has leveraged his credit and job history and transferred about $800,000 of under-performing assets into Strait Path real estate. As a result, his net worth has skyrocketed by $1,567,000 since we began investing together in 2005, and his monthly positive cash flow totals $8,377.

The Key to Path #4

Building and maintaining *momentum* is the key to path #4. The huge advantage of this path is the ease of starting. So much time and effort is eliminated at this phase.

Review: The Four Keys of the Strait Path Process

The keys to the four paths describe the overarching process that governs the Strait Path system. These four keys are summarized here:

1. **Prepare.** Believe it or not, real estate investors must be able to purchase properties. The first and most important step is to establish one's ability to do so. Some people have not had sufficient time to do this, and others have experienced setbacks that require them to start over. Such people need to put in the requisite time and effort before they can start purchasing properties. Others have been preparing over the years without being aware of it. As soon as they get plugged into the Strait Path system, they're able to move immediately to the next step.

2. **Purchase.** The next step is to start purchasing properties to generate cash flow, but more important, to build equity that can be leveraged into more deals.

3. **Leverage.** The more properties one buys and the more equity one accrues, the more able one is to leverage those assets to purchase more.

4. **Momentum.** At this stage, an investor simply has to duplicate the process to achieve critical mass and create exponential growth. I discuss this in detail in chapter eight.

The point I want to drive home here is this: *Everyone* can become a real estate investor. Everyone can participate in the Strait Path system. The question isn't who can or if you can; the only question is how long it will take based upon your circumstances. Even people in the worst financial circumstances can become wealthy through real estate investment. It may take them a bit longer, but it's unquestionably achievable.

The purpose of the portfolio game plan is to identify all your assets, and then design an achievable ten-year goal. Determine what you want to achieve and how much cash flow you need to make it happen. Then, create a plan to leverage your existing assets and resources to achieve your goal. Such a structure helps you "keep your eye on the prize" so that you can avoid the temptations of giving up or spending your cash prematurely and irresponsibly. This brings us to our next step.

> ### Strait Path Sign #2
> Develop discipline in your investing by creating a ten-year portfolio game plan. Identify current resources and assets and a desired goal, and then create a specific, step-by-step plan for achieving that goal. Having this goal in place will help you delay gratification.

To calculate what you could make in ten years on the Strait Path, visit www.straitpathrealestate.com. We've provided a simple calculator to help you see how powerful the system is and how it can help you leverage and maximize your existing assets.

ACHIEVING CRITICAL MASS THROUGH ENDURANCE

Your ten-year goal is the destination. Your passion behind the goal fuels your efforts on the path. Ultimately, it's the vehicle of repetition that gets you to the goal. Strait Path real estate is not a get-rich-quick scheme. It's not designed for people who lack discipline and persistence. It does not provide quick fixes. What it *does* provide—unlike risky schemes or traditional retirement products and strategies—is a safe and sure route to a stable retirement.

However, if you step off the path prematurely, you won't reach your destination. Underlying the system is the fundamental key of repetition. You have to duplicate the process over and over again to enjoy long-term results: purchase discounted properties, finance them to tenants through Compassionate Financing, sell them as tenants become credit worthy, and then roll the cash into the next deal until you reach your ultimate goal. The good news is that this is easy to do. The bad news is that many people don't have the discipline to do it. We refer to this repetition as "achieving critical mass," which we discuss more in chapter 8.

> ### Strait Path Sign #3
> Delay gratification by reinvesting your profits, especially in the early years. Then, "endure to the end" by repeating the investing process over and over until you achieve your goal.

Investing is a means to an end. It's a road that leads—or should lead—to an ultimate destination. As Lewis Carroll wrote, "If you don't know where you're going, any road will get you there." Without a portfolio game plan, real estate investing is like throwing stuff up against the wall to see what sticks. It's far more effective to begin with the end in mind by creating a precise, customized, and achievable plan that considers your existing resources and abilities.

Finding Investment Properties

Though my first home was valued at $150,000, I purchased it for $110,000. Before buying the property, my net worth was zero. How's that for a jump in net worth in one day? The exciting part of this stage is that you can make more money on an initial real estate investment than you can in an entire year of working. Imagine how it would feel to increase your net worth by $40,000 with the signing of a few documents. Isn't that worth learning how to find great real estate deals?

When I was just starting out in real estate, I spent countless hours combing through real estate magazines and classifieds and exploring neighborhoods in search of "for sale by owner" and listed property signs and hot deals. It took so much time and effort that I realized that it could very easily be a full-time job. It wasn't how I wanted to spend my time—I wanted to spend my time making deals and creating profits. I listened to an "expert" who said, "If you look at a hundred homes, make ten offers, get three offers accepted, and purchase one property, that's probably going to be a tremendous deal." That sounds good on paper, and he's probably right. The only problem is that it's not practical—it takes hundreds of hours to consider a hundred properties.

I knew there had to be a better way, and I set out to create it. I wanted a system that would fulfill three criteria: 1) I wanted the best deals in my area sent to me every morning like clockwork, 2) I wanted only single-family residences worth less than the median home price in my area ($250,000 at the time), and 3) each property would need to have at least 15 percent equity for me to consider it.

I developed that finding system, and the results surprised even me. After the first week of trying it out, I had four excellent deals under contract. There was only one problem—the deals kept coming. The next morning, a number of lucrative deals showed up on my desk. The morning after that, the same thing happened. I had gone from spending hours upon hours scouring the landscape to having the best deals in my area show up at my desk every morning. By this time, I had built a small team, and we were receiving about fifty solid deals per month using the finding system I had created. We quickly got frustrated with our inability to purchase more than a few homes at a time. We were letting many more deals go than we were completing. This was the birth of Real Estate Investment Companies. We realized that there were so many great deals to go around, we just had to share them with others.

In this chapter, you're going to learn the same system I've used to identify hundreds of profitable deals. There are four steps to this process: 1) define the criteria of the properties you want to look for, 2) find the properties, 3) evaluate the properties, and 4) negotiate and get the deals under contract.

Before you get ahead of yourself, however, it must be stressed that before you even start looking for properties, you need to be prepared to purchase them. This may seem obvious, but it's overlooked more often than you might think. Remember that speed is a major differentiating factor to Strait Path real estate. Being unprepared to purchase properties slows you down and may cause you to lose out on great deals.

Meet with a mortgage broker to determine exactly what you need to qualify for investment financing. Or, if traditional financing isn't an option, then you must revert to creative financing in the form of either sandwich financing or partnerships. In either case, get your ducks lined up before you start looking. Know exactly how much you can qualify for and how you're going to purchase your properties.

> **Strait Path Sign #4**
> Be prepared to purchase before you start looking.

With this preparation in place, it's time to start looking. But you must know what you're looking for.

DEFINE THE CRITERIA

Before you start looking for investment properties, there are a number of essential criteria that must be understood. These define the types of properties to look for and help you weed out a lot of time and energy wasters. They include the following:

Only Purchase Below the Median Home Price

This is one of the critical keys that set the Strait Path system apart from any other. Specifically, it's one of the core factors that help us maintain profitability and reduce risk in any market.

People always need homes regardless of market fluctuations. Buying homes below the median home price in your area provides immunity from most market volatility, for a couple of reasons. First of all, the median home price range experiences far less value fluctuation than more expensive homes. Second, if we can purchase homes at a 15 percent discount, the market will have to drop a full 15 percent before we're adversely affected, which is unlikely. (Not to mention that our buy-and-hold strategy takes care of that rare circumstance anyway.)

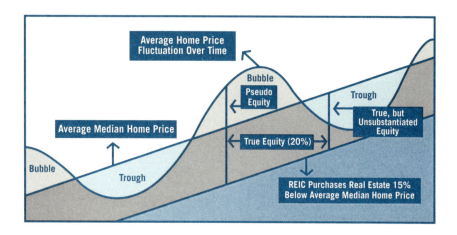

These are entry- to mid-level homes that have the most buyers. In my area, the median home price is $250,000. This number will change depending on the market you're in. You can find out the median price in your area by consulting with your city's urban development department or doing a simple online search.

Most real estate systems will tell you to buy anything that has a lot of equity. But equity in a home that won't sell is meaningless. For example, suppose the median home price in your area is $200,000. You find a home that appraises for $1.5 million, and you can purchase it for $1 million. You're blown away that you can walk into $500,000 of equity. Unfortunately, the $1.5 million price tag severely limits your number of potential buyers. It may take you six months to a year to sell the home, and possibly even longer, if ever. High-end real estate is especially risky in volatile markets and lending environments like we've experienced recently in the United States. Even with good credit and solid assets, it's extremely difficult for anyone to get such a sizable loan. Not only do you have far fewer buyers considering your home, but most of them will be eliminated by prohibitive lending requirements.

It's also important to clarify that the smallest single-family residences I buy are three bedroom, one bath homes. Again, the principle here is to deal only with the most-wanted real estate.

> ### Strait Path Sign #5
> Never purchase investment properties that are priced above the median home price in your area. Doing so significantly increases your risk by reducing your number of potential buyers. Only buy the most-wanted real estate to give yourself the best chance of selling.

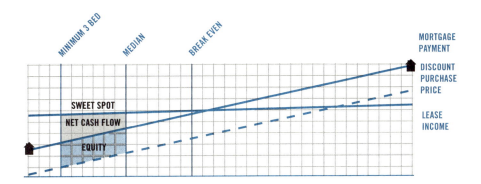

I don't care how much equity is in a home—if it's valued above the median home price for the area, I won't even consider it. I make sure that I always have the most-wanted real estate to shield myself from market risk. Equity in high-end homes is like a Pied Piper—it's a high-risk temptation that almost always leads to failure.

I have a friend who found this out the hard way. In February 2007, he and his wife purchased a home for $690,000 that they were confident was worth about $800,000. It had an unfinished basement that they knew they could finish out for about $50,000, which they felt would increase the value of the home to about $1.2 million. Murphy's Law immediately came into play. Their contractor took far longer to finish the basement than he had stipulated in the contract. By the time it was finished enough to get an appraisal, the lending market had tanked. Their mortgage broker disappeared without a trace. They were stuck with a 7,000-square-foot home and a $5,500-per-month mortgage that was drowning them financially. They couldn't refinance, and since the market had dropped, they could find no buyers. Luckily, at the last minute they found a buyer, but only after they had lost four other investment properties and $120,000 cash. They barely got what they owed on the property in the sale. What they thought was $460,000 of equity turned into a nightmare scenario that they are still recovering from.

Don't fall into this trap by straying from the Strait Path. Only purchase investment properties at or below the median home price for an area.

Purchase Only Homes That Are in Livable Condition

While equity in luxury homes is a Pied Piper, fixer-uppers are like a hamster wheel—they require tons of effort and knowledge, and you must keep doing them over and over again to continue making money. Your goal is to get a buyer into the home as quickly as possible. Homes that need a lot of repairs will drain precious time and money before you're able to do this. Buying these homes isn't investing—it's a day job. For every home you find with equity that needs major repairs, there are many others with more equity that need no repairs. The "deal of the year" comes along every day once you get plugged into the Strait Path system.

A word of caution: *livable* means different things to different people. One of the biggest mistakes I see investors make is when they walk through a house and make this judgment based on whether or not they themselves would live in the home. If the carpets and cabinets are dated they rule the home out, thinking that those items need to be replaced. But because of the Strait Path Compassionate Financing strategy, you're putting people into your investment properties that feel blessed for the opportunity. They may have negative marks on their credit, or they may not have a large enough down payment to qualify for conventional financing. They're willing to overlook wear and tear that you may be uncomfortable with because of the great benefits they're receiving, including the opportunity to own their own home and build significant equity, among many others. Relative to the benefits, dated carpet is a small price to pay for those whom the Strait Path system is designed to serve.

By *livable* I don't mean perfect and up-to-date. I mean functional. Ideally, you find homes that don't need any work at all before you advertise for tenants. However, some minor issues may be worth your time to resolve. If a home has no carpet, it needs carpet. If the water heater is broken or the roof leaks, I'll fix it. However, if the cabinet squeaks, I don't fix it. If the carpet is stained, I don't replace it—although I may have it cleaned if it's bad enough. Dated paint colors are not a problem. Basically, if you find yourself saying, "I don't like this _____ (fill in the blank) aspect of the home," you probably shouldn't fix or replace it. However, if you say, "I need to fix the _____ or the _____ won't be functional," then it should be fixed.

I will buy a home that needs minor repairs about 20 percent of the time, because the equity is too compelling. Otherwise, I rule out fixer-uppers, and I definitely avoid anything that requires more than several thousand dollars. For every good deal I find that needs a lot of work, if I use discretion and wait a bit longer, I almost always find one with just as much equity but that requires little or no work.

To help you with this process, I've created a free download that gives you a complete "Fix vs. Don't Fix" list. Download it now at www.straitpathrealestate.com.

There may be times when you bend this rule just a bit to make a home more attractive. But I strongly discourage this in most cases, for a few reasons.

First, there's a difference between the market, or appraised, value and the *perceived* value of a home, and improvements that increase the perceived value generally do not raise the market value. Contrary to common belief, the condition of a home valued at or under the median home price in an area has little effect on its market value. The expense of replacing linoleum with tile, upgrading countertops, or repainting is not justified by the new adjusted home value.

Appraiser Jack McKelvy said, "People often ask if making improvements (such as adding a garage, fence, etc.) to a home will add equal value to the home's appraisal. From an appraisal perspective, sellers probably won't get an equal return. However, improvements may add appeal that helps sell a home. The key is to make the house look nice, but it probably won't matter from an appraisal point of view."

The market value is determined by what other similar homes have sold for in the market, based on the price per square foot. The perceived value is the value that individuals assign to a home based on their perceived evaluation of its condition. For example, if a house is perfect inside, but the grass has not been cut for a year, then my perception of its value may diminish—perhaps by tens of thousands of dollars. The home may be worth less to me, but technically, the landscaping does not affect its market value. Put $300 into beautifying the lawn and my perception of its value may jump substantially. There may be even worse issues, such as worn and dirty carpet and a poor paint job, that may decrease the perceived value of the home by as much as $50,000 for certain individuals, even though the carpet and paint could be replaced for $5,000.

You may want to fix up a home to raise its perceived value and make it more attractive. However, this is usually not necessary, since our system finances homes to families who are more than happy to make improvements in exchange for the opportunity to own a home. For you, this means no property maintenance. For them, it means being able to fix up the home (with your approval). Painting and replacing dated items is a privilege unavailable to renters; your tenants will enjoy having the control to beautify the home.

And finally, with the Strait Path system, you'll sell the home based on an appraisal at the time of purchase. The appraisal will reflect the market, not the perceived, value. Buying undervalued homes and selling them later through Compassionate Financing at fair market value, not perceived value, is the key to realizing great profits in real estate. In contrast, if you were to buy an undervalued home and rent it out, its condition would probably deteriorate over time. If you sold the home in five years, you would either need to spend thousands of dollars to increase its perceived value, or you would need to discount the property. This is yet another reason why Strait Path real estate is four times more profitable than renting.

> **Strait Path Sign #6**
>
> Purchase homes in livable condition that need little to no fixing up. Making improvements to a home will usually only help you sell the home faster for the same price. Let your Compassionate Financing tenants make improvements to the home and reap the benefits as they work toward home ownership.

Some of my first tenants, Andy and Laurie, were college students when I offered them the opportunity to rent to own. Andy was working full-time and they may have been able to get approved for a loan, but they just weren't ready for such a major commitment. Rent to own was a perfect fit for them. They loved the idea of having a place they could call their own. The home was in fairly good condition, but they enjoyed fixing it up over time. The painted almost the whole interior and improved the yard. The home also had a small apartment, which they refurbished and rented out. Two years later they purchased the home, and they still live there today.

Remember that you're not buying the home for you; you're buying it for individuals and families who may see things differently than you.

Put yourself in their shoes and see things from their perspective. Once you understand just how much Compassionate Financing benefits them, you'll understand the term *livable* at a whole new level. The general rule of thumb is to put the least money and effort into investment properties as possible, while garnering the greatest returns. Eighty to ninety percent of the homes Strait Path investors purchase do not require major or cosmetic fixes prior to being resold.

FIND INVESTMENT PROPERTIES

> **How to Calculate Your Equity Position**
>
> Divide the purchase price by the estimated market value, which will give you a decimal. Then, subtract that decimal from one to get the percentage. For example: $180,000 (purchase price) ÷ $220,000 (market value) = 0.82. 1 - 0.82 = 0.18. The equity position in this case is 18 percent. By aiming for at least a 15 percent equity position on each home, you're destined to make a healthy profit.

The first rule of successful real estate investing is to buy below market value. Remember that bargain equity is the first of the five profit centers. When you buy a home for $170,000 that is worth $220,000, you increase your net worth by $50,000 immediately, versus the months and years it takes you to do the same thing through other means.

If you're like most investors, however, you probably think that it's extremely difficult, or even a matter of luck, to find good real estate deals. Or, you're tired of dealing with angry sellers after submitting "lowball" offers. Once you plug into the Strait Path, you'll never need to write such an offer. Good deals are in such abundance that you just need to learn how to tap into them.

Remember the goal is to purchase only investment properties that have at least 15 percent equity. This is another critical way to mitigate risk. If the market tanks, it has to drop a full 15 percent before you will be adversely affected, which is highly unlikely in most circumstances.

> ### Strait Path Sign #7
> Buy only homes with at least a 15 percent equity position. This is one of the most important ways to shield yourself from the risk of market downturns. The market must drop by at least 15 percent before you're adversely affected, which is extremely rare. And even if this does happen, you're never forced to liquidate at a loss.

You might be wondering if these great deals actually exist, or if they're only available to a privileged few. They do exist, as we've proven with hundreds of transactions, and they are available to anyone who knows how to find them. (And by the way, we don't look for them where investors typically look.)

In our area, about one thousand homes are listed on the market every week. Ninety percent of the homes are listed at the right price and take an average amount of time to sell. Five percent are listed too high, and they end up sitting for months until the seller lowers the price or the market gets better. Another five percent are listed below actual market value, and these are the homes that our system is designed to identify quickly. They are usually hidden from the untrained eye, but anyone can spot them easily once trained.

These below-market-value homes aren't short sales or foreclosures. So how do we find them? We search for real estate where there is the least competition. The best place to find these deals—the Multiple Listing Service (MLS)—may seem to be the most unlikely, since the MLS is so well known. The irony is that this is exactly *why* it's the best place to look—all the other investors, thinking the MLS is too obvious, are competing in other venues that appear to be less well known. The fact is that deals in these "hidden" venues are much more hotly contested, and the MLS is the most underutilized tool available to investors. Most investors don't know how to leverage the MLS at all. Through the Strait Path system, you will be able to leverage the MLS consistently and get the first dibs on the best properties as soon as they're listed.

Most important, we don't have to create deals with substantial equity by lowballing or through lengthy negotiations. We're simply not interested in 95 percent of the listed real estate. Eliminating the majority of homes makes it easier to sift through the precious few. If you consider only homes that are already great deals to begin with at their current listing price, then you are going to fulfill rule number one in real estate: to buy only undervalued properties. You'll make your money when you buy, and realize the profit when you sell.

> ### Strait Path Sign #8
> **Avoid competition from investors by staying away from common arenas, such as short sales, foreclosures, auctions, and notice of default lists, and looking for properties solely on the Multiple Listing Service.**

You, too, can learn to leverage the MLS to find the best deals in your area. A few people are unable to use our finding system, such as those in areas with extremely low populations. But for most investors, at least hundreds, and usually thousands, of homes are listed weekly on the MLS.

There are a number of reasons why people list homes for less than market value. It might be a distress sale because of extenuating circumstances, such as divorce, job loss, or a job transfer. It can also be for positive reasons. For example, I once bought a home from an individual who had recently sold his business and wanted to move quickly to his retirement home in Arizona. Whether we know the seller's story or not, we never have to offend him or her with embarrassingly low offers. What we *do* know is that the seller has set the price and is happy taking it, even if it's significantly below market value.

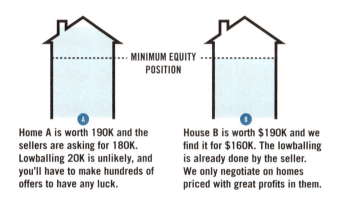

Home A is worth 190K and the sellers are asking for 180K. Lowballing 20K is unlikely, and you'll have to make hundreds of offers to have any luck.

House B is worth $190K and we find it for $160K. The lowballing is already done by the seller. We only negotiate on homes priced with great profits in them.

Whatever the reason, these homes do not last on the market. They are literally "here today, gone tomorrow" deals. Once they are identified, it's critical that we act on them immediately before we lose them. You should already be pre-qualified to purchase an investment property and have a specific plan for purchasing the home. Your success at this stage is largely a function of speed—this is precisely why you need a predicable system to help you find and analyze potential deals quickly.

HOW TO FIND DISCOUNT PROPERTIES ON THE MLS

Let me start this section by warning you that you won't find good deals by asking a real estate agent to search the MLS for you. While you should leverage the time, knowledge, and efforts of realtors, you must learn how to train them to work on your terms, and not the other way around.

I learned this lesson early on in my investing career. At the beginning of this chapter, I mentioned how much time I wasted looking for deals and how I set out to create a system with three criteria. I did, in fact, create that system, and you're going to learn how I did it in this section.

After asking myself some basic, logical questions, I created my finding system based on four realizations.

First, I knew that money is made in real estate when you buy, not when you sell. I knew that I could negotiate more equity in one day than I could expect to earn in appreciation in a few years. Finding substantial equity therefore became a top priority.

Second, I realized that the MLS would be the best place to find deals. All the real estate books I had read taught investors to drive around in search of "for sale by owner" properties, to look for notices of default, to find divorce situations, to scour short sale and foreclosure databases, to attend auctions, and so forth. I quickly realized that finding deals in these venues would require tons of time and effort, and that I would encounter fierce competition from other investors. To overcome these issues, I chose to search on the MLS. (By the way, I have purchased real estate in those competitive arenas. It's certainly possible, but it's extremely difficult to build a duplicable system around. Not to mention that it takes way too much time and effort relative to Strait Path real estate.)

Third, I knew that if I wanted to be the first to get to the best deals, I would need to leverage other people in my finding efforts. Unfortunately, I also realized that, generally speaking, most realtors aren't trained to deal with investors, nor do they know how to find deals containing at least 15 percent equity. They think it's way too much hassle to find such deals. They like deals to be "clean" and quick and prefer not to mess with "creative" options.

Fourth, I realized that what fueled realtors' aversion to investors is that most investors are big talkers but can't actually fulfill. Realtors understandably get burned out wasting time on such people, and it makes them leery of working with other investors. They do, however, appreciate investors who can identify good deals quickly and who have the ability to act on them without complication. In addition, most realtors don't believe it's possible to find homes with 15 percent equity because they don't have a system and have never done it themselves. I therefore learned that being prepared to purchase before looking is a critical, though often overlooked, step. Since I wanted realtors to help me find deals, I knew I needed to respect their time. Just as I wanted them to create value for me, I needed to offer them the same consideration.

Armed with these four realizations, I grabbed every real estate magazine and newspaper classifieds I could find and pored over property descriptions. My goal wasn't to look at real estate. Rather, I wanted to identify realtors who understood what I wanted to accomplish and would be valuable assets for me. I discovered that for every ten or eleven realtors, there would be one who would use terms and phrases, such as "great investor opportunity," "strong discount," and "high cap rate," that indicated good deals for investors.

After a few days of this, I identified ten realtors in my area who I felt would be a good fit for me and my goals. I remember the day I called them like it was yesterday. This was several months after my wife and I had purchased our first property. Since we had bought it at such a great discount, we had a lot of equity, which we extracted through a refinance. I had enough money for a down payment on another property. I was at my telemarketing job on a Saturday and had just completed all of my prospecting calls. Finding time on my hands, I pulled out my list of ten agents. I was so nervous to call them that I wrote out a script, word for word. It said something like "Hi, my name is Kris Krohn. I'm a local real estate investor. I'm prequalified to buy my next investment and put down 20 percent. After reading your listings, it sounds like you represent investors. I wanted to let you know that if you come across any good deals, I'd like you to call me, and I'll go take a look immediately. I'm looking for homes with at least a 15 percent discount." I left them with my phone number and hung up.

Here's what happened: When I gave them the 15 percent discount criterion, eight out of the ten told me something along the lines of "You're crazy! That's impossible to find." However, two of them said they'd go to work for me. Then, *both of them sent me listings that very same day.*

Although I wasn't very knowledgeable or sophisticated about real estate, I had spent time familiarizing myself with real estate pricing in my area. I had broken up the area into logical quadrants, and then studied the price per square foot of similar-sized homes in each quadrant. This trained my mind to quickly identify undervalued homes. One of the realtors sent me three listings. Based on my research, there was one out of the three that jumped out at me. It was a 3,000-square-foot home priced at $150,000. I knew that similar homes were going for about $80 per square foot, and this one was listed at $50 per square foot.

I immediately called the realtor and told him I was quite interested in that particular property. That afternoon, I drove out to the home on 1100 North 77 East in Pleasant Grove, Utah. It was a bank-foreclosed home and the bank had just listed it. Had I done the exercise the day after, it would have undoubtedly been under contract. That day, which was the first day it had been listed, the bank received three offers. One of those offers was mine, and it happened to be the best one. I bought the home quickly. I still own that home and it has increased my net worth and produced profits in excess of $106,000 over the course of five years. I've also leveraged it to purchase even more real estate.

> **The Price per Square Foot Test**
>
> To calculate the price per square foot of a home, divide the asking price by the square footage. For example, suppose you're considering a 2,400-square-foot home with an asking price of $136,000. $136,000 ÷ 2,400 = $57/square foot. This formula does not determine the market value, but it does help in recognizing potential deals. The key is to be very familiar with the price per square foot for specific homes in specific areas. This makes it very easy to spot potential deals when you receive lists from realtors.

That was the exciting part. The disappointment came when I asked the realtor to keep bringing me properties, but he was unable to duplicate the process. He didn't have a system in place; he had just gotten lucky that day. I found this to be common. Not only do realtors not have duplicable systems, they each have varying personal opinions about real estate values and processes, which further adds to their inability to repeat the process of finding investment properties.

When I was ready to purchase my next property, I started from scratch again. I grabbed the real estate magazines and examined the listings to identify ten more realtors. I called these next ten and had the same experience: eight of them told me I was crazy, two said they'd work for me, and one of them sent me a listing that became my next deal.

Although individual realtors couldn't duplicate the results, my research system did. And, after all the time and research, the success of the system boiled down to one thing: speed. If I could create a replicable system to access the best deals on any given day, I knew I'd be able to snatch them up before anyone else.

> ### Strait Path Sign #9
> Leverage the time and resources of realtors by having them find deals for you.

Now, Real Estate Investment Companies has a complete in-house system that finds deals every day, often within minutes of them being listed on the MLS. We've become so familiar with the market and available listings that all we do now is check new listings as they come up. This yields us a couple great deals per day, and these deals are given to our investors to purchase.

Here are the main points to learn for you to duplicate the finding system in your area:

- Don't look for properties—look for realtors instead. Find every outlet for real estate advertisements in your area. Search them to identify at least ten realtors who use key words that indicate that they work with investors, or at least that they focus on deals with equity.

- Once you've identified ten realtors, call them and tell them what you're looking for, and that you're qualified and ready to buy (assuming that's true), and ask them to call you when they find deals with your specifications. Expect that the majority of these realtors will think you're crazy, but one or two of them will be willing to work with you.

- Understand that it's not agents that will yield good deals—it's the market. Agents only help you locate what the market is yielding. You need to make your specifications and investment modes very clear to your realtor(s) so that they work on your terms, rather than you catering to how they like to work. Being prepared and willing to move quickly on the right deals will make for a good relationship with them.

- Familiarize yourself with your area so that you can pick out good deals quickly. Focus only on homes priced below the median home price in your area. Know the average price per square foot for various home sizes and layouts. The evaluation process is covered in detail in the next section.

- When you identify homes with at least 15 percent equity, move on them immediately. Go to the home as soon as you've determined it's a good possibility. Use the negotiation method you'll read about in this chapter, and then make an offer. Remember that the essence of the finding system is speed. The deals you'll find through this system will be gone within days after being listed, and usually within one day. You'll have the chance to do due diligence, but you first need to get them under contract as soon as possible.

The next step teaches you how to evaluate deals when realtors send them to you, as well as how to train realtors to duplicate finding the best deals for you.

HOW TO EVALUATE POTENTIAL INVESTMENTS

You've found a property that you think has great investment potential. You know you have to act fast, but you want to make sure that the deal is solid. At this point, utilizing a proper evaluation process is critical. The evaluation process consists of a comparative market analysis and a walk-through visual inspection.

Before I explain these, it must be understood that there is really only one way to determine a property's true value, and that is to sell it. (Remember, however, that ours is a short-term buy-and-hold strategy that usually lasts two to five years. We aren't interested in selling immediately; we just want a close approximation of the current market value.) But because our system operates on speed and we buy homes before typical investors get to them, we must do our best to ascertain the value through comparisons.

A comparative market analysis, or CMA, is an informal appraisal that helps you determine the value of the home so you can make sure it holds enough equity. Contrary to common belief, a CMA provides a much more accurate market value than do purchase appraisals, because of a few reasons that I detail in the next chapter. Performing a comparative market analysis consists of three main steps:

1. Locate all possible comparables on the Multiple Listing Service through your real estate agent.

2. Choose which properties apply from the list that is generated through your search. The goal is to narrow down the list to the most relevant three to five properties.

3. Estimate the market value of the subject property.

Step 1: Locate All Possible Comparables

After your realtor has sent you a potential investment, you're going to ask him or her to generate a list of comparables. You should identify every possible comparable property in that region. This first list will include really great and really poor comparables. The selection process comes after this step; at this point you're just generating a list of all possibilities.

For your initial list, you want to find properties that have sold in the last six months within a ten-block radius of the subject property. Generating this list requires access to the Multiple Listing Service, which is one reason why I recommend that you work with a realtor.

Step 2: Identify the Most Relevant Properties

There are eight core factors that determine relevance with comparables: 1) square footage, 2) bedrooms and bathrooms, 3) layout (single-story, two-story, basement, rambler, etc.), 4) year built, 5) location, 6) what percentage of the home is finished, 7) the sold price, and 8) the listing date. Obviously, the most relevant comparables are those that most closely match your subject property in all eight of these areas. It's critical that *you* choose these properties, rather than your realtor, at least until he or she is trained in the system. Few realtors will know how to choose the most relevant properties.

Here are the guidelines for each factor:

1. **Square Footage:** Square footage comparisons should be kept within 15 percent of each other. For example, on a 2,000 square foot home, only compare homes between 1,700 and 2,300 square feet (at least when possible).

2. **Bedrooms and Bathrooms:** If the subject property has two bedrooms, you can compare two- to three-bedroom homes. If it has three bedrooms, you can compare three- to four-bedroom homes. If it has four bedrooms, you can compare four- to five-bedroom

homes. For bathrooms, you don't want more than one full bathroom discrepancy. As you become familiar with market values in your area, you'll find that there's a much greater jump in value when you go from a three-bedroom to a four-bedroom home than when you go from a two-bedroom to a three-bedroom home. Going from four bedrooms to five doesn't make a significant difference. The more you study real estate, the better you'll understand. We recommend that investors purchase only single-family homes with three bedrooms or more.

3. **Layout (or Type of Home):** The ideal comparison has the same layout as your subject property. However, in some cases this may be impossible to find. When forced to compare different layouts, you must make allowances in your final figures to compensate for the differences. For example, all other factors being equal, a basement home will be worth less than a two-story home. You can't stretch layout comparisons too far. For instance, you can get away with comparing a single-level home to a split-level, but you can't compare it with a three-story home.

> **Free Video: How to Perform a CMA**
>
> It's difficult to describe the market analysis process in a book. To make it as understandable as possible for you, we've created a video that walks you through the process, step by step. Access it now at www.straitpathrealestate.com.

4. **Year Built:** The newer the home, the closer your comparables need to be to the year built. The older the home, the larger the discrepancy you can allow. For example, if I'm considering a home that was built in 2005, I probably won't compare it to any home built prior to 2000. On the other hand, if the subject property was built in 1980, I'll consider anything built between 1970 and 1990.

5. **Location:** Ideal comparables are within ten square blocks of your subject property.

6. **Finished Percentage:** This factor usually refers to a basement, though not necessarily. You should only consider properties that are within 20 percent of the completed percentage of the subject property. For example, if the basement in your property is 85 percent complete, you can compare properties having basements that are 65 to 100 percent complete.

7. **Sold Price:** If a home sold for less than its listing price, that tells you it was probably listed too high. Conversely, if a home sold for more than its listing price, it was probably listed too low. Also, if the subject property is listed at $180,000 and a comparable sold for $300,000, the chances are high that there are major differences between the homes.

8. **Listing Date:** This factor becomes important when you start to fine-tune your projected market value after the MLS generates a potential market value. For example, if a comparable home sat on the market for eight months, that's a sign that it was probably priced too high. On the other hand, if a home sold within thirty days, it was probably listed below market value.

After considering each of these eight factors on every property on your list, narrow it down to the most relevant properties, with a minimum of three comparables.

Step 3: Determine the Market Value

Once you've identified at least three relevant properties (the more you can find, the more accurate your end value will be), the next step is to project the market value. Have your realtor use the MLS to do this. Input the most relevant comparables along with the subject property, and run the report on the MLS called the "Comparative Market Analysis," which will calculate the market value for you based on every relevant factor.

Once you have an estimated market value from the computer, you must use human logic to ascertain how accurate the value is. In some cases, I may choose to adjust the market value based on my knowledge of the market, the specific area, and/or anomalies with the home.

Suppose I'm considering an entry-level home that is offered at $120,000. I find four relevant comparables in the same development, all of which have the same square footage, the same number of bedrooms and bathrooms, the same layout, and the same construction year as the subject property. All four comparables sold for $180,000 within the last six months. In this case, I can be reasonably certain that the unit I'm considering has about $60,000 of equity. My next step is to determine whether there's something wrong with the property. If I can't disqualify it, then I'll move on it and make an offer.

That's a simple example. It gets complex when you're working in neighborhoods for which it is difficult to find relevant comparables, or if a home has unique features that cannot be compared with other properties. The less information you have, and the less relevant your information, the more you're forced to extrapolate data through reasoning and educated guesses. For example, I once purchased a home in a neighborhood that had sold very few homes in the previous years. It was a popular neighborhood for professors of a nearby college, so people didn't move often. When homes were listed in the area, they sold quickly, but they were very rarely listed. So I was forced to extrapolate. Luckily, I knew enough about the area that I felt confident about my decision, and it turned out to be a great deal.

Consider the following two examples, which I pulled from the Multiple Listing Service. The first sheet for each example is the subject property, followed by a list of comparables, and ending with a sheet showing the most relevant comparables along with the subject property, and an estimated value of the subject property.

Example 1:
This subject property is a 2,072 square foot, three bedroom, one and a half bathroom rambler with a full walkout basement listed at $179,900. It was built in 1954.
Notice that this home is priced below the median home price in my area, which is critical. Notice that the bedrooms and bathrooms also meet the guidelines for Strait Path real estate.

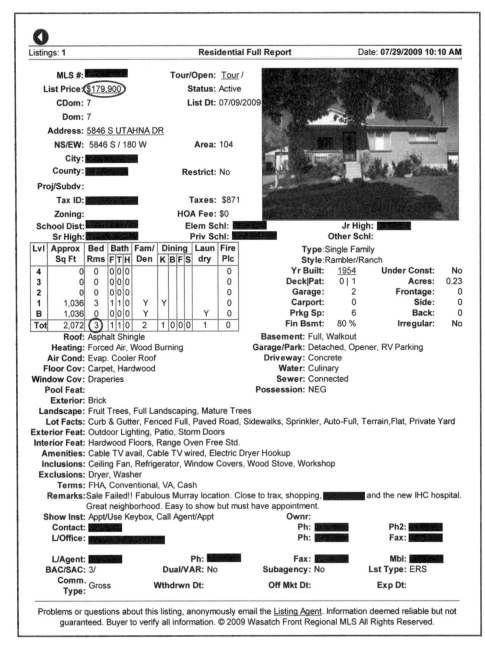

FINDING INVESTMENT PROPERTIES 119

Now let's consider a few sold comparables from the Multiple Listing Service.

#	MLS/Address	Price	Status	Type	SqFt/Acres	Sold Price	DOM/Tour
1.	846805 / 769 WILLOWOOD AVE / 4/2.00/1 0/2	$244,900 / FULL/35%	SLD	Rambler/Ranch / 11/14/2008 12/08/2008 1961	2,484 0.20	$237,000 / 6265S/769E / SNGL	13 / Tour / 1
2.	808573 / 6013 NOVA DR / 4/2.00/2 1/0	$217,900 / PART/90%	SLD	Rambler/Ranch / 06/13/2008 12/31/2008 1953	2,298 0.16	$200,000 / 6013S/65W / SNGL	14 / Tour / 1
3.	847906 / 403 E SAUNDERS ST / 3/2.00/2 0/1	$199,900 / FULL/90%	SLD	Rambler/Ranch / 11/19/2008 01/27/2009 1953	1,736 0.18	$199,900 / 5450S/403E / SNGL	15 / Tour / 1
4.	735758 / 4030 S 500 E / 4/1.00/1 3/0	$260,000 / PART/90%	SLD	Bungalo/Cottage / 09/27/2007 03/03/2009 1939	2,076 0.72	$180,000 / 4030S/500E / SNGL	16 / NA / 1
5.	840135 / 322 E CLARK ST / 3/2.00/1 2/0	$309,900 / NO/CR/0%	SLD	Rambler/Ranch / 10/13/2008 04/07/2009 1950	2,267 0.32	$300,000 / 4800S/322E / SNGL	17 / Tour / 11
6.	856509 / 4867 CENTER ST / 4/2.00/2 1/0	$239,500 / FULL/100%	SLD	Bungalo/Cottage / 01/12/2009 04/13/2009 1952	1,966 0.23	$232,500 / 4867S/180E / SNGL	18 / Tour / 11
7.	858290 / 5833 S UTAHNA DR / 5/2.00/2 1/0	$200,000 / DYLT, ENTR, FULL/97%	SLD	Rambler/Ranch / 01/19/2009 04/13/2009 1954	2,320 0.19	$193,000 / 5883S/180W / SNGL	19 / Tour / 4
8.	839948 / 5763 LINDON ST / 4/2.00/2 2/0	$205,000 / FULL, WLKO, OTHR/100%	SLD	Bungalo/Cottage / 10/14/2008 04/14/2009 1949	1,810 0.20	$201,300 / 5763S/177E / SNGL	20 / Tour / 7
9.	833212 / 315 E HILLSIDE DR / 5/2.00/2 1/2	$239,900 / DYLT, FULL/100%	SLD	Rambler/Ranch / 09/16/2008 04/24/2009 1955	2,208 0.25	$231,000 / 5440S/315E / SNGL	21 / Tour / 12
10.	846016 / 5560 S 235 E / 4/2.00/1 2/0	$249,900 / DYLT, ENTR, FULL/100%	SLD	Rambler/Ranch / 11/08/2008 04/24/2009 1961	2,400 0.19	$236,500 / 5560S/235E / SNGL	22 / Tour / 1
11.	867999 / 7 W VALLEY DR / 3/2.00/2 1/0	$199,900 / FULL, SHLF, WLKO/0%	SLD	Rambler/Ranch / 03/03/2009 04/30/2009 1952	1,790 0.17	$199,000 / 6300S/7W / SNGL	23 / Tour / 12
12.	883689 / 5357 KNOLLCREST ST / 4/2.00/2 1/1	$250,000 / FULL/100%	SLD	Rambler/Ranch / 05/07/2009 06/15/2009 1948	2,040 0.34	$253,000 / 5357S/370E / SNGL	24 / Tour / 6
13.	877075 / 378 E 6230 S / 5/3.00/1 1/0	$204,500 / FULL/95%	SLD	Rambler/Ranch / 04/09/2009 06/17/2009 1962	2,064 0.18	$212,000 / 6230S/378E / SNGL	25 / Tour / 1

1. We'll eliminate this comparable because the square footage is not within 15 percent of the subject property.
2. This comparable isn't ideal because it sold too long ago.
3. This is a great comparable.
4. This house is too old relative to the subject property.
5. We'll eliminate this home because it doesn't have a basement, unlike the subject property.
6. We could use this one if we didn't have better options, but it's too far away from the subject property to make an ideal comparable.
7. This home has too many bedrooms.

8. This is an ideal comparable.
9. This home also has too many bedrooms relative to the subject property.
10. The square footage on this home does not fall within the 15 percent range; it's too big.
11. This home has a basement, but it is not finished.
12. This is an excellent comparable.
13. Again, too many bedrooms.

Now we take the three best comparables from the sheet above and place them alongside the subject property (first column) to generate an estimated market value.

CMA Report for:

	Subject	COMP 1 - RMBL		COMP 2 - BNGL		COMP 3 - RMBL	
Address:	5846 S UTAHNA	403 E SAUNDERS ST		5763 LINDON ST		5357 KNOLLCREST ST	
	SUBJECT - RMBL						
MLS #:	n/a	Adj Factors	847906	Adj Values	839948	Adj Values	883689	Adj Values
Status:		Sold		Sold		Sold	
List Price:	Med: $121k-$200k	$199,900		$205,000		$250,000	
Sold Price:		$199,900	199900	$201,300	201300	$253,000	253000
DOM:		48 days		182 days		19 days	
Sale Date:		01/27/2009		04/14/2009		06/15/2009	
Apprec:		2 %	183 days	2004.48	106 days	1169.19	44 days	609.97
Bedrooms:	3	1000	3 beds		4 beds	-1000	4 beds	-1000
Full Baths:	1	3500	1 F bath		1 F bath		2 F bath	-3500
¾ Baths:	1	2500	1 ¾ bath		1 ¾ bath		0 ¾ bath	2500
½ Baths:	0	1750	0 ½ bath		0 ½ bath		0 ½ bath	
L4 SqFt:	0	30	0 sq ft		0 sq ft		0 sq ft	
L3 SqFt:	0	30	0 sq ft		0 sq ft		0 sq ft	
L2 SqFt:	0	30	0 sq ft		0 sq ft		0 sq ft	
L1 SqFt:	1036	35	868 sq ft	5880	1,012 sq ft	840	1,140 sq ft	-3640
Bsmt SqFt:	1036	10	868 sq ft	1680	798 sq ft	2380	900 sq ft	1360
Bsmt % Fin:	80 %	12	90%	571.2	100%	369.6	100%	-854.4
Total SqFt:	2072		1,736 sq ft		1,810 sq ft		2,040 sq ft	
$/Sold SqFt:	$109/sqf		$115/$124		$111/$115		$124/$115	
Year Blt:	1954	500	1953-56 yrs	500	1949-60 yrs	2500	1948-61 yrs	3000
Garage:	2	2500	0 cars	5000	2 cars		1 cars	2500
Carport:	0	750	1 cars	-750	0 cars		1 cars	-750
Misc. Feat.:								
Misc. Feat.:								
Misc. Feat.:								
	Ave Adjusted Value		Adj. Total	214786	Adj. Total	207559	Adj. Total	253226
	Print	**$ 225,190**						

1. Note that the comparables are within ten square blocks of the subject property.
2. They all have the same or comparable layout.
3. They are all within one bedroom and one bathroom of each other.
4. They all have basements, and the finished percentages are all within 20 percent of each other.
5. The square footage of each home is within a 15 percent range of the subject property.
6. The year built on each home is within ten years of the subject property.
7. Based on our relevant comparables, the estimated value of the home is $225,190. It's currently listed at $179,900, which gives us just over a 20 percent equity position.

Example 2:
This subject property is a 2,210 square foot, four bedroom, one and a half bathroom, multi-level home with a partial daylight basement listed at $219,900. It was built in 1961.

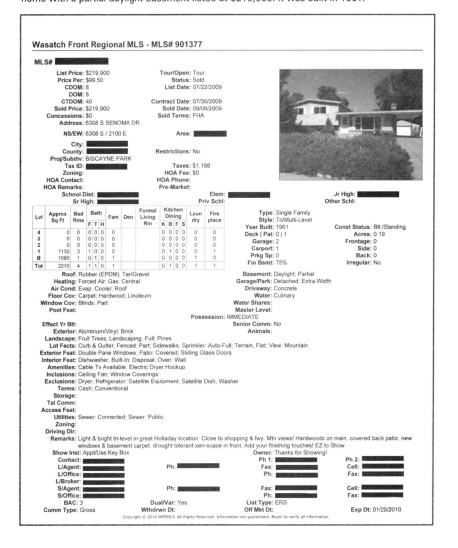

Wasatch Front Regional MLS -

Photo	MLS # Address Bd/Bth/Fm	List Price Gar/Port	Status Bsmt/%Fin	Style City, State List DT	Tot SqFt Sold DT	Sold Price Acres Year Blt	Actions NS/EW Type	Tour/Open Photo Cnt
1.	847961 6556 S 2475 E 3/2.00/0	$249,900 0/2	Sold Entrance; Partial/90%	Tri/Multi-Level 11/19/2008	1,700 01/21/2009	$240,000 0.25 1959	6556 S / 2475 E Single Family	Tour 10
2.	839789 2490 DOLPHIN WAY 5/3.00/2	$269,000 2/0	Sold Partial/90%	Tri/Multi-Level 10/13/2008	2,150 02/18/2009	$261,000 0.27 1960	7830 S / 2490 E Single Family	Tour 12
3.	854951 7120 S 3080 E 3/2.00/2	$239,900 2/0	Sold Daylight;Walkout/50%	Tri/Multi-Level 01/05/2009	1,849 02/25/2009	$237,500 0.21 1960	7120 S / 3080 E Single Family	Tour 7
4.	858694 6446 S SUMAC WAY E 3/2.00/1	$224,000 1/0	Sold Daylight/90%	Tri/Multi-Level 01/20/2009	1,750 02/26/2009	$224,000 0.25 1960	6446 S / 1400 E Single Family	None 4
5.	842880 6492 S LOMBARDY DR 4/2.00/1	$269,000 2/0	Sold Full/100%	Tri/Multi-Level 10/23/2008	1,650 03/04/2009	$273,000 0.22 1959	6492 S / 1410 E Single Family	Tour 12
6.	854783 3537 E HONEYCOMB RD S 4/3.00/2	$259,600 2/0	Sold Partial/100%	Tri/Multi-Level 01/02/2009	2,116 03/27/2009	$240,000 0.24 1968	7800 S / 3537 E Single Family	Tour 1
7.	837185 2093 E HAUN AVE 5/2.00/1	$249,900 2/1	Sold Partial/65%	Tri/Multi-Level 09/29/2008	2,590 04/08/2009	$230,000 0.18 1961	6350 S / 2093 E Single Family	Tour 12
8.	855239 2786 E COVENTRY LN S 3/3.00/2	$249,900 1/0	Sold Partial/100%	Tri/Multi-Level 01/06/2009	2,099 04/24/2009	$230,000 0.18 1974	7465 S / 2786 E Single Family	Tour 10
9.	873668 7062 S 1935 E 3/2.00/2	$204,900 0/2	Sold Daylight; Partial/100%	Tri/Multi-Level 03/26/2009	1,666 05/11/2009	$199,000 0.21 1960	7062 S / 1935 E Single Family	None 1
10.	869988 1141 E HYLAND LAKE DR S 3/2.00/2	$238,500 0/2	Sold Partial; Walkout/90%	Tri/Multi-Level 03/11/2009	1,960 05/20/2009	$225,000 0.23 1958	5880 S / 1141 E Single Family	Tour 3
	882187 6478 S SUMAC WAY E 4/3.00/2	$259,000 2/0	Sold Entrance; Full/100%	Tri/Multi-Level 05/01/2009	1,850 05/28/2009	$250,000 0.19 1959	6478 S / 1325 E Single Family	Tour 11
11.	843174 7351 N TREE DR 4/2.00/2	$269,000 2/0	Sold Full/40%	Tri/Multi-Level 10/29/2008	2,152 06/01/2009	$263,000 0.22 1973	7351 S / 3340 E Single Family	Tour 10
	878604 6505 S HICKORY LN E 3/3.00/1	$262,000 2/2	Sold Entrance/95%	Tri/Multi-Level 04/16/2009	1,800 07/03/2009	$262,000 0.19 1959	6505 S / 1460 E Single Family	Tour 11

1. The square footage on this comparable is too low relative to the subject property.
2. This home is too far away from the subject property.
3. The finished percentage of the basement on this home is too low.
4. The square footage on this home is also too low.
5. Again, this home is too small to be a good comparable.
6. This home is also too far away.
7. This home is too big.
8. The subject property is more than ten years older than this home.
9. This home is also too small.
10. These three are our most relevant comparables in this scenario.
11. This home is also too new relative to the subject property.

CMA Report for: Carma Needham

Address:	6308 S SENOMA		1141 E HYLAND LAKE S DR		6478 S SUMAC E WAY		6505 S HICKORY E LN	
	SUBJECT - TLVL		COMP 1 - TLVL		COMP 2 - TLVL		COMP 3 - TLVL	
MLS #:	n/a	Adj Factors	☑ 869988	Adj Values	☑ 882187	Adj Values	☑ 878604	Adj Values
Status:			Sold		Sold		Sold	
List Price:	Med: $121k-$200k		$238,500	225000	$259,000	250000	$262,000	262000
Sold Price:			$225,000		$250,000		$262,000	
DOM:			14 days		11 days		4 days	
Sale Date:			05/20/2009		05/28/2009		07/03/2009	
Apprec:		2 %	64 days	789.04	56 days	767.12	20 days	287.12
Bedrooms:	4	1000	3 beds	1000	4 beds		4 beds	
Full Baths:	1	3500	2 F bath	-3500	1 F bath		1 F bath	
¾ Baths:	1	2500	0 ¾ bath	2500	2 ¾ bath	-2500	1 ¾ bath	
½ Baths:	0	1750	0 ½ bath		0 ½ bath		1 ½ bath	-1750
L4 SqFt:	0	30	0 sq ft		0 sq ft		0 sq ft	
L3 SqFt:	0	30	0 sq ft		0 sq ft		0 sq ft	
L2 SqFt:	0	30	650 sq ft	-19500	625 sq ft	-18750	600 sq ft	-18000
L1 SqFt:	1130	35	638 sq ft	17220	600 sq ft	18550	600 sq ft	18550
Bsmt SqFt:	1080	10	672 sq ft	4080	625 sq ft	4550	600 sq ft	4800
Bsmt % Fin:	75 %	12	90%	2462.4	100%	2220	95%	2880
Total SqFt:	2210		1,960 sq ft		1,850 sq ft		1,800 sq ft	
$/Sold SqFt:	$115/sqf		$115/$120		$135/$139		$146/$149	
Year Blt:	1961	500	1958-51 yrs	1500	1959-50 yrs	1000	1959-50 yrs	1000
Garage:	2	2500	0 cars	5000	2 cars		2 cars	
Carport:	1	750	2 cars	-750	0 cars	750	2 cars	-750
Misc. Feat.:								
Misc. Feat.:								
Misc. Feat.:								
	Ave Adjusted Value		Adj. Total	235801	Adj. Total	256587	Adj. Total	269017
Print	**$ 253,802**							

Notice again that our subject property falls within the median home price in this particular area. All of these homes are within ten square blocks of each other, they have the same layout, they're within one bedroom and one bathroom of each other, the finished percentages of the basements are within 20 percent of each other, the square footage is within the 15 percent range, and their age is within the ten-year range.

Based on our comparables, the estimated market value of this home is $253,802. Since it's listed at $219,900, we can feel fairly certain that there is about 13 percent equity in the home. Since our minimum equity position at purchase is 15 percent, I would negotiate to get the price down to our minimum to create a greater margin of safety.

Here's the number one rule of performing accurate CMAs: The more you extrapolate (or make educated guesses) and the more standard deviations you allow, the more conservative your projections need to be. As a further caution, you want to avoid guesswork as much as possible. There comes a "tipping point" where you have to guess so much on a property that you should probably avoid it, no matter how good of a deal it seems. You've got to be certain that you're determining the most accurate value as possible—by finding the most relevant comparables—for the Strait Path system to work.

Speaking of finding the best comparables, in my efforts I realized that this was where realtors were falling short, which was why they weren't able to duplicate the process. They would locate potential comparables but then not know how to identify the most relevant properties.

Suppose you're looking in a very specific geographic area for comparables. Your search brings up thirty potential properties. You can organize these in order from the most expensive to the cheapest, and then begin to whittle down the list to the five most relevant properties. In any such search, you're going to have outliers on both extremes. On the low end, you'll find properties that were short sales, foreclosures, and rip-roaring deals for one reason or another. These are not appropriate to choose to determine the subject property's CMA. If you're choosing only five homes out of forty to average together to arrive at an accurate market value, it doesn't make sense to use anomalies. Short sales are not typical. On the other end of the scale, neither is it appropriate to use the most expensive homes, because these will also not reflect the average you're looking for. You have to pick the ones in the middle.

I found that realtors tended to use the most expensive properties when performing analyses in order to show higher values than were justified. They may have been trying to help me, but this didn't serve my purposes. The point is that I had to train realtors to perform CMAs like *I* wanted them done. Until then, they couldn't find the best deals consistently. Don't trust your agent to do what you need him or her to do without first giving guidance. If you don't train your realtors in a precise fashion, you'll find that they will work on their own terms, which probably won't be compatible with your purposes.

After arriving at a projected market value that you feel comfortable with, the next step is to see whether the home should be disqualified by performing a walk-through visual inspection to check as many components of the home as possible. This doesn't happen until after a home is under contract—your first priority is to secure the deal (see the next section). Once it's under contract, you can still take your time to make a judicious decision and ensure that there are not major issues with the home. Specifically, you'll want to examine such things as the foundation, roof, heating and air conditioning units, plumbing, cosmetic aspects, and appliances, among others. Look for major red flags that will require a lot of money and/or effort to fix. Remember the definition of a "livable" home.

NEGOTIATE

The traditional way to negotiate on real estate is to write a Real Estate Purchase Contract (REPC), have your realtor submit it to the seller's realtor, wait a few days for them to respond with a counteroffer, and then go back and forth until you've settled on the price and terms. For example, suppose you find a home that you think is worth $200,000, and it's listed for $195,000. You offer $180,000. Two days later, they counter with $190,000. You counter with $185,000 a day later, and then after a few rounds of this you settle on $187,500. To arrive at a final, accepted offer may take a week, or even longer.

This is a total waste of time. If we used traditional negotiations with our Strait Path deals, we would lose nearly every one. The deals we find are so hot that if we don't get them under contract within the first day or two that we hear about them, we have to compete with a number of competitive offers that roll in.

Therefore, we use a very clear and firm negotiating strategy to ensure that this doesn't happen. We are honest and up front. We don't play games or attempt manipulation. In fact, our strategy is a nonnegotiating strategy.

We don't need to play games, lowball, or go back and forth with tedious counteroffers because we consider only properties with at least 15 percent of substantiated equity anyway. That's the first and most important step to a quick and easy negotiation process.

In fact, if a home is listed at 15 percent below market, I strongly discourage investors from asking the seller to go much lower. If I find a home that I'm certain is worth $200,000 and the seller is asking $170,000, I'm not going to offer $150,000 just to see how low the seller will go. In the first place, I think it's wrong, and second, it increases my chances of losing the deal. In such circumstances, think of how you would feel making a lowball offer in person. If you would feel guilty or embarrassed, you're probably not doing the right thing. Furthermore, you'll probably lose the deal.

One of the best and most honest things you can do in real estate is consider only those homes that have built-in equity, rather than trying to create equity through lengthy negotiations. So many would-be investors find homes with small amounts of equity and then offer significantly less than the asking price. They then tend to burn out after writing hundreds of these lowball purchase contracts that don't go anywhere. The only thing they accomplish is upsetting sellers. There's absolutely no reason to offend anyone with the Strait Path real estate system.

After identifying a deal, we have our real estate agent call the listing agent to find out as much information as possible about what the seller is willing to accept as an offer. If there's enough equity in the home and/or the seller is willing to be flexible, our next step—before we submit an offer—is to call the seller's realtor and verbalize our offer. We explain that this is our highest and best offer and that we will only write one contract. We make it clear that we are not emotionally attached to the home but that we are extremely prequalified and serious.

Only after receiving a verbal acceptance or counteroffer over the phone will we consider writing an offer. Thus after finding out as much as possible, we write an offer that we know has a high likelihood of being accepted. Upon submitting it to the seller's realtor, we explain again that this is our highest and best offer and that the seller should strongly consider not counteroffering.

Here's a sample conversation between one of our agents and a selling agent.

> **Your realtor:** Hi, I'm calling on behalf of my client about a home you have in Branbury. Is it still available?
>
> **Selling agent:** Yes, it's available. It just hit the market.
>
> **Your realtor:** I see it's listed for $120,000. How flexible is your client?
>
> **Selling agent:** He's a little flexible, but it's priced right.
>
> **Your realtor:** My client is prequalified and ready to put 20 percent down on a home. He's interested in a few homes but isn't looking to pay more than $115,000 with some concessions. He acts fast and doesn't want to waste time with offers and counteroffers. Is $115,000 and some concessions a possibility, or should we check out other prospects?
>
> **Selling agent:** Actually, I think my client would consider an offer like that.
>
> **Your realtor:** I'll send an offer if you think your client will go for it. We really don't have a lot of time for counteroffers. If we write it up this hour, can we get a response by tonight or tomorrow morning, worst case?
>
> **Selling agent:** I'll have a response by tonight.

Using this strategy cuts days from what is usually a lengthy and time-consuming process, but it can be intimidating to some. Some people fear that they will lose properties. But if you're using the right finding strategy, you never have to worry about losing properties. If a seller is unwilling to contract with you, you'll have plenty more excellent deals to consider.

To review, here are the steps of Strait Path negotiations:

1. Begin negotiations only on homes with asking prices that reflect at least 15 percent equity.

2. Ascertain as much information from the seller as possible in order to write a deal with a high likelihood of being accepted.

3. Arrive at a verbal agreement before you submit a written offer.

4. Appropriately posture yourself so that sellers understand that you won't go back and forth—you're giving them your absolute best offer.

> **Strait Path Sign #10**
>
> Eliminate wasted time in the negotiation stage by cutting to the chase and avoiding tedious counteroffers.

Once you have a deal under contract, your next step is to perform due diligence and purchase the home. Congratulations! At this point, you're very close to a substantial increase in your net worth.

Purchasing Investment Properties

"The most important thing for a young man is to establish credit—a reputation and character."

—John D. Rockefeller

The purchasing process is one of the most critical aspects of real estate investing. It is extremely complex and, at times, stressful. For these reasons, investment lending is definitely not a do-it-yourself game. You need a broker who can navigate you through the complexities and pitfalls, and get your deals closed.

In this chapter, I won't detail everything there is to know about investment lending. However, I will equip you with the knowledge you need to choose the right mortgage broker, since this is one of the most valuable members of your investment team. I'll also provide you with the most important guidelines to follow in the world of financing. If you follow these guidelines, and then choose the right mortgage broker and let him or her handle the complexities, you'll be able to grow and optimize your real estate portfolio. The guidelines are as follows:

- Understand how to qualify for loans.
- Understand the purpose of a purchase appraisal.
- Become profit-conscious, versus rate-conscious.
- Finance multiple properties and protect your future portfolio by selecting the right broker and loans.
- Manage your debt-to-income ratio through Compassionate Financing.

HOW TO QUALIFY FOR LOANS

As I've mentioned, the financing process should begin before you even start looking for properties. You need to know exactly how much you can qualify for so you can know how to direct your property search. This step will save you a lot of time and effort down the road, as well as those you work with, including realtors and lenders. It's an extremely painful experience to go through the hassle of finding and getting a property under contract, only to get denied for the loan.

There are many factors that determine your creditworthiness. For the sake of simplicity, I'll only touch on the most important, which include your credit score, income, job history, and debt-to-income ratio.

Credit Score

Your credit score measures your credit risk level. Created by the Fair Isaac Corporation, it is also referred to as a FICO® score. It tells lenders how likely you are to pay them back on time. Credit scores range from 300 to 850, and the higher your score, the more likely you are to get financed and the better your loan terms. Credit scores are calculated based on your rating in five general categories, which include your payment history (35 percent), amounts owed (30 percent), length of credit history (15 percent), new credit (10 percent), and types of credit used (10 percent). (Source: www.myfico.com).

Depending on your game plan and the current market, credit scores between 600 and 800 are the most useful. We recommend that investors strive to maintain a credit score of 700 or higher. We have access to loan programs that will approve individuals with scores as low as 580, since the market is struggling. However, the terms on these loans are worse than if your credit score is higher. To understand your credit score and learn how to improve it, visit www.myfico.com/CreditEducation.

Income

Obviously, the higher your income, the more, bigger, and better loans you can secure. However, remember that on the Strait Path we only purchase properties at or below the median home value in any particular area, which means that it doesn't take a lot of income to get approved for these deals. For example, one of my clients purchased a home while making just $13 an hour.

Job History ? 2 Pay Stubs?

Lenders want to see that you're stable, that you're not jumping around from job to job, or from industry to industry. Their rule of thumb is to require loan applicants to show at least a two-year job history in one industry. At times it may be worth it to stick with a job you don't like for the overall good of building your portfolio.

Debt-to-Income Ratio

One of the most critical factors in lending is your debt-to-income ratio. The higher your debt relative to your income, the harder it is to secure loans. You may earn $4,000 per month, but if you have a $1,500 mortgage, a $400 car payment, and $300 in credit card payments each month, you have a 55 percent debt-to-income ratio. Ideally, you want your ratio to be less than 50 percent.

For many investors, working on these factors is their very first step, and it's something they do long before they actually buy an investment property. If you're not creditworthy now, don't wait to improve your credit worthiness—start *immediately*. If you're young and haven't yet established credit, secure two or three credit cards and develop a history of paying them off monthly. Even if you have enough cash to buy a car, it may be wise for you to keep your cash in the bank, finance a car, and then pay your loan from your liquid cash. The idea is to establish a history of securing loans and then faithfully paying them back. If you have a poor credit history, there are many companies that can help you improve your score. Another helpful step would be to create and season an LLC, or legal business entity. A legal entity that shows income can be used on mortgage applications to increase your ability to purchase more properties.

> ### Calculate Your Debt-to-Income Ratio
> 1. Add the total monthly payments of all your debts.
> Total: _____
> 2. Divide the total by your total monthly income.
> 3. The resulting fraction is the percentage of your debt relative to your income.
> Example: Total monthly payments on all debts (mortgage, auto loans, credit cards, etc.) = $1,800. Total monthly income = $5,000. $1,800 ÷ $5,000 = 0.36 = 36% debt-to-income ratio.
>
>

My little brother Nik is working on these steps now. A twenty-one-year-old college student, Nik has acquired two credit cards, which he pays off monthly. Although he could have paid cash for a car, he financed one instead in order to build credit. He has already created an LLC, which will eventually be used to substantiate business income to help him qualify for real estate loans.

I'm also a good example of the importance of building credit. My investing process started fourteen months before I bought my first home. I knew I wanted to invest in real estate, but I was a young college student with little credit history and a short job history. I learned what I needed to do to get approved for loans and started on it right away. I already had a credit card, but I knew that I needed to establish more credit. I applied for three more cards and accepted the two best offers. Then, I started using them to pay for things that I would normally pay for from my checking account, and each month I paid off the cards in full. Though there were times when I was seriously tempted to quit my job, I stuck with it because I saw the bigger picture of what a two-year job history could help me accomplish. Sometimes I would wonder why I just didn't go the traditional route of getting school loans and thus being able to enjoy my college years more, but I trusted that the sacrifice would eventually be worth it. Sure enough, because I stayed at my job long enough, I was able to personally purchase a dozen properties before graduating from college.

> ### Strait Path Sign #11
> Always be planning ahead by improving your creditworthiness in the present. Specifically focus on raising your credit score and income, developing a stable work history, and managing your debt-to-income ratio.

UNDERSTAND YOUR PURCHASE APPRAISAL

Once you have a home under contract and you've performed a walk-through inspection, it's time to secure a purchase appraisal. Be aware that an appraisal will almost always render a lower value than you determined in your comparative market analysis, for a number of reasons. Appraisals do not give an accurate market value—they simply give you a reflection of what you're trying to accomplish with the bank. There are actually different types of appraisals, and each one serves a different purpose.

At least 95 percent of purchase appraisals come in at the listing price, regardless of the actual value of the home. With every financed investment purchase, there are three parties that are trying to reconcile: the investor, the appraiser, and the bank. Each party has a different agenda. Since banks provide the money, they have the most say in this process. Their purpose is to detect loan fraud. They want to see an appraisal close to the listing price because major discrepancies between those two figures are red flags. If an appraisal comes in too low, they won't give you the loan. If it comes in too high, they worry about double contracts, which are a common form of fraud. In fact, if your appraisal is more than 10 percent higher than the listing price, they will probably demand that you disclose this fact to the seller and have them write a letter to the bank explaining why they're selling their home for far less than it appraises for. As you can imagine, this can jam up the process. *Ultimately, the purchase appraisal confirms to the bank that the home is worth at least what you are paying for it, not what the home is actually worth.*

Because of such strict regulations, appraisers are actually required to throw out any comparables that show a 10 percent difference in price as compared to the home being purchased. Appraisers must meet rigorous requirements to become certified. Because the industry is so regulated, their agenda is to produce an appraisal that will satisfy banks. Your property could be the deal of the century, but this probably won't be reflected in your appraisal. Don't be discouraged if your appraisal comes in lower than you hoped for. I'm happy when appraisals come in somewhere between my comparative market analysis value and the listing price. Because of my short-term buy-and-hold strategy, I don't view appraisals as validation of home values; I have already done that with my handcrafted CMA. Appraisals are only valid for three to six months anyway, and since I usually hold properties for a couple of years or more, I don't derive a lot of value from appraisals.

Appraisal regulations can have significant impact on fix-and-flip homes, but they are not a major factor in the Strait Path system. Not only are appraisers unable to show values much higher than purchase prices, but they are also bound by time. It's unlikely that they will give you an appraisal for $200,000, and then turn around and appraise the same home for $280,000 in two months, no matter how much work you've put into it. That would send a red flag to the bank. In fact, this is one of the major factors that makes flipping so risky—it's predicated on you making a profit quickly, and lending regulations make it extremely difficult for you to substantiate large increases in home values in the timeline you need.

Since Compassionate Financing is a buy-and-hold strategy, you don't need to worry about your appraisal coming in much lower than the market value determined by your comparative market analysis. The main point here is this: Don't be scared away from deals by low appraisals. Remember that the purchase appraisal only confirms to the bank the value they want to see for specific purposes, and your CMA is a much more accurate reflection of a home's actual market value. Know the market, perform accurate research, trust your research and your CMA, and then use Compassionate Financing to hold your property two to five years. The appraisal will accurately reflect the market value when you sell to your tenants.

PROFIT CONSCIOUS VS. RATE CONSCIOUS

Limited and misguided financial paradigms result in less than 2 percent of Americans being financially independent by age sixty-five. This is made apparent when it comes to interest rates on loans, particularly mortgage loans. We, as a country, have become terribly rate conscious because of our fear of consumer debt. Most people ignore almost every other aspect of loans and place ultimate importance on their interest rate.

Here's a secret unknown to most people: *Higher interest rates can make you more money than lower rates*. Does that shock you? Allow me to explain.

Investors keep their eyes on the profits. They focus on what they gain by buying a home, as opposed to consumers who focus primarily on interest rates and what they lose by acquiring a home. Through Strait Path real estate, you're able to purchase multiple homes, but this can't happen if your sole or primary expectation is to get the best interest rates. This secret is really quite simple: The more flexible you're willing to be with your loans, the more loans you're able to secure. Your goal is to purchase as many homes as possible, not to maximize the profits of one or two deals. Interest rates are just a small part of this bigger picture. The difference between a great interest rate and a bad interest rate impacts your profit margin by less than a few percent over time. This is especially true when you consider that interest rates affect your cash flow, and cash flow represents less than 7 percent of your total profits.

We choose banks in a manner that ensures we can leverage as many homes with an investor's credit as possible. Profits of each investment home increase your net worth by six figures. Accordingly, we use banks that charge steeper rates in exchange for the privilege of purchasing more homes. They charge higher rates because they calculate that the more properties you've financed, the greater your risk of default. In the case of the Strait Path system, this isn't true, but you're playing by the bank's rules. This may mean that you trade a 1.5 percent higher interest rate for an additional $100,000 in profit, which is obviously more than worth it. The issue isn't your interest rate—it's how many banks you can get to continue lending for your portfolio.

Get Prequalified Now
Find out how much real estate you qualify for now by visiting www.straitpathrealestate.com.

One of my clients, Daren, was a high-level corporate executive when we met. He had a high net worth and income, but he realized that he needed to diversify his investments, which were largely held in the stock market. Leveraging his income and credit score, he was able to purchase five homes in one year. The interest rate on his first home was 6.75%, which generated a positive cash flow of $590 per month. On his second home, the interest rate jumped to 7 percent, with a monthly cash flow of $629. His third home was financed at 7.5 percent with a monthly cash flow of $540, the fourth was at 7.78 percent and cash flowed $550 per month, and his fifth home was financed at 8.25 percent and produced a monthly cash flow of $386. Although his interest rates continued to climb with each additional purchase, he was still profitable. Because he focused on the profits rather than the interest rates, he now cash flows $2,695 per month, he received $25,590 in up-front option considerations, and his net worth jumped by more than a quarter of a million dollars just from his initial purchases.

> **Strait Path Sign #12**
>
> When financing your investment homes, keep your eye on the profits, not on your interest rates. Use the banks that allow you to purchase the most real estate, not those with the lowest rates.

FINANCE MULTIPLE PROPERTIES AND PROTECT YOUR FUTURE PORTFOLIO WITH THE RIGHT BROKER AND LOAN

One of our secrets to rapidly acquiring so many homes is understanding how the banking industry works. Banks decide whether or not to accept your next purchase based on what mortgages are already on your credit, how quickly they were acquired, what banks they are with, how your profile was submitted, and what you are doing with the properties, to name just a few criteria. Our formula for leveraging several homes on one person's credit requires us to use banks in specific combinations, so that each additional bank will follow and accept more investment purchases. As a result, we can buy twice as much real estate than would otherwise be possible.

As I mentioned, I won't detail the entire formula here. The takeaway for you is this: Find the right mortgage broker who knows how to work with investors. Specifically, you don't want a broker who focuses primarily on rates; you want one who is experienced in financing multiple properties on one person's credit. Our in-house brokerage, Strategic Lending, has this expertise and experience, and may be a good fit for you.

Strait Path Sign #13

Choose a mortgage broker who specializes in working with investors and who is experienced in financing multiple properties on one person's credit, rather than those who focus on interest rates.

Strait Path Sign #14

When negotiating, ask the seller to pay your mortgage broker's closing fees. Our recommendation is to ask the seller to pay 2 percent, which means that the broker can make his or her fees on the front end and will likely not increase your interest rate on the back end of the loan to ensure they get paid. Having the seller pay 2 percent toward your loan fees typically means that you get the net rate the bank can afford. This gives you the lowest debt-to-income ratio and the best cash flow.

The right broker will know how to use the right combinations of banks and to submit files in the right way to help you secure multiple loans. Equally important is choosing the right loans. When the goal is to maximize your portfolio, you can't get just any loan. You need to utilize specific loan programs that increase your ability to purchase multiple properties. These include more creative and flexible options than fixed loans, such as Adjustable Rate Mortgages (ARMs). Keep in mind that our goal is to control properties, not pay them off. Using traditional loans severely limits your leveraging power. And, once again, the best way to handle this is to work with a suitable broker.

HOW TO CHOOSE THE RIGHT MORTGAGE BROKER

When choosing your mortgage broker, use the following criteria:

1. More than 50 percent of their experience and current loan volume should be working with investment products.

2. They should close at least thirty loans per year to remain knowledgeable of current products.

3. They should have put at least five homes on one person's credit and duplicated this with at least five people.

4. They should have access to a minimum of twenty banks with investment products.

If you have trouble finding a broker who meets these criteria, I invite you to consider our in-house broker, Strategic Lending (www.strategiclending.net).

> ## Strait Path Sign #15
> Maximize your portfolio by utilizing flexible loan programs.

There's a reason why we take such pains to choose the right mortgage brokers and loans: we're looking ten years down the road, not just at immediate purchases and strategies. When people secure loans in a hodgepodge fashion—getting one loan here and another there, using this broker now and that broker later—it unravels their ability to purchase as much real estate as possible. We caution our clients to leave their entire lending business with professionals who can foresee complicated lending issues, and who have the ability to fix any past mistakes. We're thus able to solve and dodge potential issues long before they arise.

One key to this foresight is creating LLCs and/or corporations immediately. Corporations both protect you from liability issues as well as increase your ability to finance more real estate. With the proper documentation and long enough seasoning, banks will allow you to secure loans with your corporation, instead of just your personal name. We help our investors set up "series LLCs," which are comparable to corporations with several subsidiaries. A series LLC allows you to place each investment property in its own entity without having to set up a new entity with each purchase. We set these up as soon as possible, since we understand the long-term benefits of doing so.

And, of course, in addition to setting up liability protection, you should also do everything in your power to improve your credit. I can't stress enough how important it is to cultivate a long-term perspective. This is precisely where so many people fail. Their inability to see down the road prevents them from taking appropriate action now. Then, when they look in the past at their failure, they're left with the wistful thought "If only." Avoid regret by thinking and planning ahead.

> **Strait Path Sign #16**
>
> Plan ten years ahead when financing investment properties. Protect your future portfolio by making wise lending decisions. Leverage the knowledge of a competent, investor-oriented mortgage broker to accomplish this. Also, be aware of how you can increase your future chances of getting financed, including setting up and seasoning corporations, and improving your credit.

OPTIMIZE YOUR DEBT-TO-INCOME RATIO THROUGH COMPASSIONATE FINANCING

One of the major advantages of our hybrid system, Compassionate Financing, over rentals is that our system optimizes your debt-to income ratio. Banks will typically recognize only 70 to 75 percent of rental income to account for vacancies. In other words, suppose you have a rental property with a mortgage payment of $1,000, and you receive $1,200 per month in rent. Most banks will count only $900 as rental income, which means that rentals negatively affect your debt-to-income ratio. If your total monthly debt is ever 50 percent or more of your monthly income, you will no longer qualify for real estate loans.

With Compassionate Financing, you can collect about $200–300 more per month than you would by renting (not to mention the up-front option consideration fee). This compensates for lending guidelines and optimizes your debt-to-income ratio. In the scenario above, let's say that you collected a monthly payment of $1,400, rather than $1,200. Seventy-five percent of $1,400 is $1,050, which means that even after the bank accounts for vacancies, your debt-to-income ratio is actually improved (or lowered), relative to renting. You're showing greater monthly income than liability, and your debt-to-income ratio has improved by 5 percent per month.

This means that you'd probably be limited to one or two rentals, versus being able to purchase multiple properties with Strait Path real estate.

> **Strait Path Sign #17**
>
> Optimize your debt-to-income ratio and increase your ability to finance more investments by using Compassionate Financing, as opposed to renting out your properties.

BEYOND THE LOAN: THE FULL PURCHASE PROCESS

Closing on a property is a big enough hassle in and of itself. But how can you be sure that you've bought the right property? How can you protect yourself from buying a real estate "lemon"? There are seven specific steps to give you peace of mind, which are as follows:

1. Walk-through visual inspection
2. Professional home inspection
3. Seller's disclosures
4. Home warranty
5. Insurance policy
6. Placing the property into an LLC
7. Compassionate financing contract

While these steps are not all necessary, they provide layers of protection that can make your investment more secure. Together with your financing process, these constitute the full purchasing process requisite to buying the right properties.

Walk-Through Visual Inspection

Your personal walk-through visual inspection occurs before your potential investment is under contract. Because you're finding excellent deals, it's critical that you contract them as soon as possible. But a visual inspection is an excellent opportunity to discover any red flags.

Don't waste your time with a superficial inspection—be thorough. Look for major issues, such as a leaking roof, inoperative appliances, a cracking foundation, a broken air conditioner, and so forth. Remember, however, that you are an investor. You must view the property through your "investor spectacles." Look past dated cabinets, dingy carpets, and chipping paint on the walls. The home does not need to be in perfect condition to qualify as a perfect prospect for a Compassionate Financing client.

Professional Home Inspection

Professional home inspections examine structural and mechanical components of your home, including the foundation, grading and drainage, roof and roof structure, interior and exterior walls, ceilings, floors, doors, windows, fireplaces, porches and decks, electrical systems, heating and cooling systems, plumbing systems, water heaters, built-in appliances, garage doors and operators, doorbells, dryer vents, smoke alarms, sprinkler systems, pools, and spas. Professional inspectors identify catastrophic flaws in the structural or mechanical components of a home, and point out minor issues that could give you long-term trouble if they are not addressed.

Every property will have flaws. You want to protect yourself by finding them, but common flaws should not deter you from purchasing a home. They may even give you leverage to negotiate a lower sale price, and some sellers may even be willing to fix the issues themselves.

A professional home inspection is not always necessary, especially because the Strait Path liquidation strategy ultimately makes your end buyer responsible for any issues that may arise with the home. However, a professional inspection may help you create more peace of mind.

Seller's Disclosures

Seller's disclosures are listed in a multipage form that sellers are required to give to buyers stating all the physical problems and defects that the sellers are aware of. Sellers are required by law to disclose any "defects in the property known to the seller that materially and adversely affect the value of the property that cannot be discovered by a reasonable inspection by an ordinary prudent buyer." If you do discover that the sellers intentionally withheld information regarding something wrong with the property, rest assured that you have grounds for legal recourse with the help of your realtor.

Mandatory disclosures offer you, the buyer, another layer of protection. However, note that this only applies to problems that sellers know exist. If an issue arises after purchasing the home and you suspect that the seller knew about it and failed to disclose it, you must prove it in court. This is why these disclosures should always be accompanied by a walk-through inspection and/or a professional home inspection.

Home Warranty

The National Board of Realtors describes home warranties as "service contracts, typically lasting one year, that cover the repair or replacement of major home systems and appliances that break down due to normal wear and tear." Home warranties protect homeowners from repair costs that aren't covered by home insurance. They cover such things as plumbing, heating, air conditioning, and major appliances. In some cases, the warranty may extend to garbage disposals, doorbells, ceiling fans, garage door openers, water softeners, trash compactors, and built-in microwaves.

They don't cover pre-existing appliance problems or structural problems. Home warranties cost about $200 to $400 a year, as well as $35 to $50 for service calls. Most warranties last one year before expiring.

Because of the way we sell properties, I very rarely purchase a home warranty; through Compassionate Financing, our end buyers handle all property maintenance. However, if you can negotiate for the seller to provide a home warranty, then by all means do so. Otherwise, it's not necessary.

Homeowners Insurance Policy

Homeowners insurance provides financial protection against disasters. Unless you are buying a home with cash, you will be required to secure an insurance policy. Standard policies cover both the home and items within the home. They may also provide liability protection. Damage caused by most disasters is covered, although there may be exceptions, such as floods, earthquakes, and poor maintenance. Make sure that you buy the most comprehensive policy possible. In my area, most insurance policies do not cover mold. I always add mold coverage into my policies, and this has saved me considerable heartache through the years. For example, a pipe once broke in one of my properties and mold started growing within a few days, before the insurance claims adjuster arrived. Seventy-five percent of the house ended up being redone on the insurance company's dime because I had insisted on mold coverage when it wasn't the standard.

With Compassionate Financing, this premium policy is escrowed into the home and lumped into the payment. Tenants are responsible for the deductible, if used.

Protect Yourself Through an LLC

We recommend that investors place each investment property in a Limited Liability Company (LLC) or other legal entity. Such entities distance your personal finances from the properties and protect you in the event of lawsuits. If you are ever sued for any reason, plaintiffs may only pursue assets that are in your name. Properties placed in LLCs are immune to legal action against you personally. Individuals *can* sue specific LLCs, but as long as you have each property in a separate LLC, only the targeted property is at risk; the others are kept safe.

Another reason we urge investors to use LLCs and corporations is to help with financing down the road. If you use a separate bank account for an LLC and keep good accounting records, banks will let you use the LLC to get approved for more properties. However, legal entities used for financing must be "seasoned," meaning that they must exist for a certain time period, usually about two years. There's a limit to how many properties you can finance in your name. But if you can present a seasoned LLC with verifiable records to a bank, you can exponentially increase your ability to purchase properties.

Compassionate Financing Contract

The REIC contract is probably your best assurance in this entire process. According to our contract, any and all problems become the responsibility of the tenant following an initial ten-day inspection period. During that period, the tenant has the opportunity to test all major systems in the home. For example, if the water heater is broken or the furnace is out of order, we agree to come in and fix the problem. After the ten-day grace period has passed, such responsibilities are turned over to the tenants.

Rest assured that these seven tools will protect you well against a "lemon" property. By incorporating them into every deal, I have never run into any trouble with the hundreds of homes purchased by me or by any of my clients. Let's now explore Compassionate Financing, which is your best form of protection.

Compassionate Financing: Profit Through Service

"Everything about business comes down to people. Where in business can we escape the impact of human care, human creativity, human commitment, human frustration, and human despair? There is no reason for anything in business to exist if it does not serve the needs of people."

—Bruce Cryer

Compassionate Financing is the heart and soul of the Strait Path system. There are many other important components to the system, but this is the core that everything else revolves around. As such, it's the most important thing you can learn about successful real estate investing.

Compassionate Financing is a type of seller-financing program that provides the benefits of lease options while eliminating their flaws. A lease option is a lease agreement with the option to purchase the home under the terms of the agreement. They are designed as gateways to home ownership for renters, who suffer from the following disadvantages:

- Renters have little to no control over pre-existing conditions.
- Rental property repairs are often slow.
- Renters are not building any equity.
- Renters do not benefit from the appreciation of property values.
- Renters may have to pay for property improvements.
- Renters cannot build credit through renting.
- Renters must tolerate their neighbors.
- Renters must deal with common walls and the associated noise.
- Often, no pets are allowed in rentals.
- Rent per square foot is high, which translates into small bedrooms and living areas.
- Renters have limited choice and influence over surrounding environments, school districts, and location.

Almost everyone prefers home ownership to renting. However, many people are unable to qualify for traditional financing. In fact, recent data shows that 32.2 percent of Americans rent. (Source: http://www.postchronicle.com/cgi-bin/artman/exec/view.cgi?archive=75&num=153861). Because of strict lending requirements, applicants can get rejected for weak documentation or below-average credit scores. People in such positions can either rent until they can improve their financial situation, or obtain seller financing on a home. A lease option is a hybrid form of seller financing. Buyers, or tenants, can benefit from lease options in the following ways:

- The buyer can make improvements and feel at home.
- The buyer gains time to improve his or her credit.
- The buyer can often build equity faster than he or she can with conventional financing.

- The buyer may be able to acquire a seasoned loan since he or she has been living in the home.
- The buyer can walk away from the home with no liability.
- The buyer can get into a home with a relatively small amount of money.
- This transaction does not show up on the buyer's credit.

In theory, lease optioning gives first-time homebuyers and people who are unable to get traditional financing the opportunity of home ownership. However, lease options have developed a bad name in the industry because of how many investors use them. Investors like lease options because they can collect an option consideration (down payment) up front, as well as charge a higher monthly payment than if they were renting a home. Buyers are willing to pay these fees because of the opportunity to purchase the home. However, if the tenant does not purchase the home in the time frame stipulated by the agreement, then the investor can evict the tenant, and then bring in another tenant under the same agreement.

In other words, lease options can become predatory and exploitive. Many lease-option tenants end up not being able to purchase the home and thus lose thousands of dollars, and when the term is over, they are in a worse position to buy a home than before. Misguided investors actually hope that their tenants do not purchase their homes because they want to keep cycling tenants through to collect ongoing down payments and higher lease payments. They create win-lose transactions, which are obviously unsustainable.

Strait Path real estate provides a much better way. Compassionate Financing is the product of years of experience and thousands of hours of extensive legal research. It has been perfected, and we have not altered our lawyer-written and -approved contracts in years. Compassionate Financing not only better serves tenants, but it is also more profitable for investors. The core difference between traditional lease options and Compassionate Financing is that we *want* our tenants to purchase our homes.

In fact, we do everything in our power to help them do so. Our system provides tools and resources for tenants to improve their credit and optimize their financial situation so that they can qualify for traditional financing as soon as possible. This creates a win-win scenario—investors love it because it's much more profitable than other forms of real estate, and tenants love it because it's an opportunity for home ownership that is otherwise unavailable.

On an even deeper level, Compassionate Financing is a triple-win transaction, the third winner being the community at large. Generating a higher level of home ownership fosters a greater sense of responsibility, improves neighborhoods because of the pride of ownership, and decreases crime and conflict within communities. Our goals extend far beyond making profits for ourselves—we want to serve individuals, families, and communities. We want to give people opportunities that they can't find elsewhere. After all, this is the best way to generate long-term, sustainable profits; those who serve the most, receive the most. When Compassionate Financing is executed well, investors are more profitable, individuals and families are in much better financial positions, and the health of the community is improved.

Austin, one of our Compassionate Financing clients, had a great job and good credit but was unable to qualify for a mortgage simply because he hadn't worked in the same industry for at least two years. Austin was sick of renting. One day he saw one of our "Rent-2-Own" signs and called on it. He was excited to learn that through our program he could earn thousands of dollars of equity, buy a home, and build even more equity in that home than a bank would ever allow. He put $7,000 down to lower his monthly payment a little and entered into an agreement with us. A year and a half later, he bought the home with over $20,000 of equity. I turned a great profit on the deal as well, and for very little effort.

Another of our tenants, Pat, didn't have enough income to qualify for a typical loan. I reviewed his situation, and although I was slightly worried about his low income, I decided to offer him a property. It turned out to be a great decision because not only was he a great tenant, but he also recently approached us to purchase the home. After three years of renting, his financial situation had drastically improved. He's now buying the home with 20 percent down, and he's also gaining the $17,000 of equity that has accrued.

One of our investors, Tyler, had an experience that demonstrates how Compassionate Financing touches lives. He had a home available that he was advertising as a rent-to-own property. He was approached by a family who had experienced financial difficulties. They explained that their daughter—one of five children—was terminally ill and that they had incurred substantial medical bills. Furthermore, Tyler's advertised home was right across the street from some of this family's relatives. They wanted to be close to family and friends for support as they dealt with their daughter's illness. When Tyler explained the program to them, they were ecstatic. They couldn't believe that it was possible for them to control a home, live in it as if it were theirs, build equity, make improvements, and all without having to get approved for traditional financing. What made the deal work for them was the flexibility. Without our program, they would have been forced to rent and would not have been able to live close to their family. Tyler worked with them and met their needs during a very difficult time. He received a $5,000 down payment, and they have faithfully paid their rent for over a year.

Not every Compassionate Financing tenant needs the program because of financial difficulties. For example, tenants Garen and Stacy are self-employed. Although they are doing fine financially, they were struggling to get approved through banks because of their work status, so our program worked perfectly for them. Flexibility is a key component of Compassionate Financing. It's so valuable to the community because it fills needs and niches that banks are unwilling or unable to cater to.

The Benefits of Compassionate Financing

For Investors

1. Immediate increase in net worth
2. Bargain equity increases cash flow
3. Collect $200/month above regular rent
4. Collect $3,000–$7,000 nonrefundable down payment
5. Collect property appreciation
6. No property maintenance
7. Property improvements (made by tenant) common
8. Lowers debt-to-income ratio
9. Tax savings
10. Save 6 percent on realtor fees when home sells

For Tenants

1. Gateway to homeownership
2. A place to call home
3. Build significant equity
4. Build equity faster than with a mortgage
5. Not throwing rent money away
6. Can make home improvements
7. Able to repair credit
8. Loan prequalification
9. Loan preparation
10. Incentives to prepare for loan qualification

ELEMENTS OF A LEASE OPTION CONTRACT

Our Compassionate Financing contract improves drastically on traditional lease options through a number of revolutionary elements. However, before these are detailed, let's cover the basic moving parts of a lease option contract, which include the following:

- Option consideration (or down payment)
- Lease payment
- Purchase price
- Length of lease
- Credited consideration (or bonus equity)
- Accumulated option payment (monthly principal)

These moving parts are negotiable and offer flexibility for both investors and tenants. For example, one person may put less down and have a little higher lease payment, while another may put more down to bring the monthly payment down.

Option Payment

An option payment is what a buyer-tenant agrees to pay a seller to make the contract with an option to purchase legal. Traditional financing on a home purchase requires money down, and at Strait Path we also require our clients to put anywhere from $3000–$10,000 down on our homes. This up-front payment offers you additional assurance that your tenant will behave wisely. If he or she breaks the terms of the contract, he or she runs the risk of losing the option payment. It's important that the contract stipulate that this is an option payment, not a down payment to be "credited" toward the purchase price. The law views the term *credit* as the tenant having equity in the home, and if you use this language, a judge could declare that your tenant does, indeed, have an equitable interest in the home.

Lease Payment

The lease payment is the monthly amount paid by the tenant. Providing tenants with the option to purchase the home allows you to charge a higher lease payment than you can generally receive in rent. I require lease payments be paid on the twenty-fifth of each month; this allows me to apply the lease payment toward my mortgage payment, which is due at the beginning of the month.

Purchase Price

The purchase price is what the tenant agrees to pay for the home when he or she exercises the purchase option. This price can be set at the time the lease contract is signed, or the buyer may agree to pay market value at the time the option is exercised, as determined by an appraisal.

Length of Lease

While a rental agreement is usually twelve months, you can write up a lease option for any time frame. If you are going to have a contract that is longer than one year, we recommend you write the contract for one year, with options for the buyer to renew the contract if certain criteria are met. We recommend a twelve-month contract with a twelve-month renewal clause in order to provide true value for our clients, many of whom need a longer period of time to correct some of the issues that have kept them from previously qualifying for financing.

Credited Consideration

By offering bonus equity, or bonus consideration, tenants can be incentivized to sign a contract. When your client goes to purchase the home, any bonus equity will be deducted from the purchase price. Sometimes a home needs a little work and you may offer $5,000 of bonus equity because of the sweat equity they may put into the home. Maybe your client is so happy about the opportunity that they don't need any bonus equity to seal the deal. This is a negotiating tool to be used at your discretion.

Accumulated Option Payment

When you pay your mortgage, a portion of the payment is applied to your principal balance. Likewise with a lease option, a portion of payments made on time may be credited to the lessee's equity in the property. This is another powerful incentive to encourage timely payments. For some contracts nothing is credited, but for other contracts this can often be up to $200 a month. We technically refer to this additional credit or equity as "additional option consideration."

REIC Investor Tyler Shares His Experience with Compassionate Financing

"I have been a landlord for a couple of rentals for the last five years. Last December, one of my renter's leases was expiring on December 31, so I decided to try the Compassionate Financing program. I hired REIC on the second week of December to sell the contract, and they had it sold and the contract closed by the last week of December. I had a new tenant before my old tenant's lease had expired! Not only that, but the contract included a $7,000 option payment and $1,550 monthly payment, which gives me $400 positive cash flow.

"During my previous days as a landlord, I was constantly involved in the maintenance of the property, which required A/C and plumbing repairs, lawn maintenance, snow issues, etc. My renters were calling me all the time. Since converting my rental property to Compassionate Financing, I not only have positive cash flow, but my total communication with the tenants has been nothing but two text messages in seven months. They are on track to purchase the property at the end of the term, which will give me enough equity to expand to more properties after that."

WHAT SETS COMPASSIONATE FINANCING APART FROM LEASE OPTIONING?

As mentioned before, lease optioning sounds great in theory, but it's often flawed in practice. Statistically, very few lease-option tenants are able to exercise their option to purchase, or in other words, to get approved for traditional financing. This means that they lose their option payment and the additional monthly amount above what they would have paid in rent. While this may benefit individual investors, in the long run it doesn't serve buyers and the community, which makes it ultimately unsustainable and unworthy of quality-minded investors.

Another flaw of lease optioning is that it automatically sets up a win-lose purchase transaction when the purchase price is set up front: either the tenant or the investor will lose when (or if) the tenant purchases the home. When you sign a lease-option contract, you have no idea what the market will do in a year's time. If you set the purchase price at the current market value and the market skyrockets during the term of the lease, then the investor loses out on appreciation. Conversely, if the market drops, then the tenant loses.

Compassionate Financing utilizes three differentiating components to eliminate these flaws, which are as follows: 1) flexible purchase price, 2) bonus equity, and 3) financing assistance for tenants.

Flexible Purchase Price

When selling a lease option, we do not settle on a future sales price up front. It can be difficult for just about any individual to guess what the market may do. Even though it goes up over time, we do not know what a consistent rate will be. The sales price in our contracts contains a "floor" with no "ceiling." The floor is the purchase price plus 75 percent of the difference between the purchase price and the CMA value at the time the contract is signed. This means that, no matter what the market does, we will never sell the home for a loss. The ceiling is determined by a fair market appraisal when the purchase option is exercised. Once the appraisal determines the value of the home, we deduct the tenant's option payment, monthly equity, and bonus equity to derive a true purchase price. For example, suppose I buy a home with a CMA value of $240,000 for $200,000. When I sign a deal with a tenant, I stipulate that $230,000 is the lowest I'll sell the home for. ($40,000 is the difference between the purchase price of $200,000 and the CMA value of $240,000. Seventy-five percent of $40,000 is $30,000.) In this example, the worst-case scenario is that I'll profit by at least $30,000. This strategy protects me from a down market, ensuring that I'm never forced to sell at a loss. On the other hand, if the tenant purchases the home in three years and it appraises at $250,000 when he or she buys, I can reduce that amount by the tenant's option payment, bonus equity, and whatever monthly credit I may have been giving him or her.

> **Protection from Market Volatility**
>
> Strait Path real estate offers more protection from market downturns than any other system, both for investors and tenants. If the market tanks, we can allow tenants to wait it out until it is beneficial to them. Also, in down markets homes below the median price are generally the most shielded from losses and often continue to appreciate when the higher-end market loses value.

Notice that with this clause we control what we can. We cannot control the market so we don't try to. But we can control the amount of equity and incentives we offer our tenant-buyers.

Bonus Equity

We encourage you to generously credit your tenants between $2,500 and $5,000 of equity because with the Strait Path system, you are saving 6 percent in realtor's fees and you are selling the property for the true market value and not the perceived value, which helps you maximize your profits. We do not typically set any prepayment penalties on a home for a premature purchase, which offers nice flexibility to the tenant. If he or she believes the market will go up dramatically the next year, he or she can try to buy it ahead of time to capture some of the appreciation.

Also, keep in mind that tenants' accumulated option consideration is credited toward the purchase price when they purchase. For example, suppose a contract stipulates that $200 per month will be applied toward the purchase price. If a tenant leases the home for two years before purchasing, and all of his payments are on time, then $4,800 will be deducted from the purchase price. (Note that we only credit on-time payments. For example, if a tenant had been late on two payments, then $4,400 would be credited.)

Financing Assistance

We want our tenants to purchase our homes. It makes their lives better and makes us more profitable. It's the only sustainable way to run a lease-option-based program. We're much more profitable if our tenants actually purchase our homes because of the principle of velocity; the more homes we buy, the more money we make.

Real Estate Investment Companies has an entire in-house program dedicated to helping tenants improve their financial situations and put themselves in a position to purchase a home. This includes financial management courses, helping them repair their credit to boost their scores, and providing them with a personal finance coach. Individual investors can create similar programs, though having it set up institutionally does streamline the program and make it easier to deliver. We encourage Strait Path investors to help their tenants in the following ways:

- Connect them with a mortgage officer who will act as their financial "coach," helping them take the necessary steps to become qualified for a loan.
- Connect them with a credit repair company. You can even include any associated costs in your contract.
- Provide them with a list of websites that teach them how to budget and save.
- Give them ongoing resources, tips, and advice through monthly newsletters.

HOW TO EXECUTE COMPASSIONATE FINANCING

The process of Compassionate Financing consists of the following three steps: 1) marketing, 2) qualifying applicants, and 3) executing contracts.

Marketing

After closing on your investment property, you want to get it under contract with a tenant as soon as possible. You also want to spend as little money on marketing as possible. Following our system will enable you to secure a tenant quickly, and with minimal expense and hassle.

The primary secret to marketing a rent-to-own property is in the signs. It really is as simple as that. You put up signs on the property and let the calls come streaming in. You're probably thinking that this is too simple and that it won't work. The truth is that there is a specific way that your signs should be made, and specific locations on the property where they should be placed. Every investment property should have at least five signs, consisting of three "Rent-to-Own" signs, one "For Sale" sign, and one "For Rent" sign. Placing these signs strategically drives the most traffic.

The focus of your marketing efforts is to generate leads, or to get as many people calling on your signs as possible. You want people in all situations to call you—those that want to just rent, those that want to rent to own, and those that want to purchase a home outright. Our program caters to all types of clients.

Your "Rent-to-Own" signs should be made like the examples below. Make sure that they are readable and laminated.

Your "For Rent" and "For Sale" signs can be the basic signs that you purchase at a home improvement store.

The following diagram shows where to place your signs for maximum visibility.

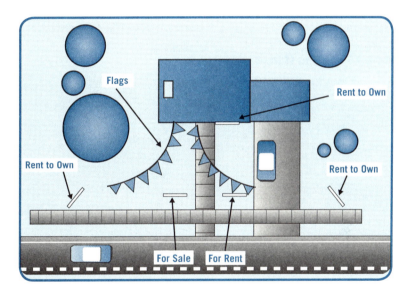

If your home is in an area that doesn't receive much traffic, there are a few other ways you can market, including advertising in free classifieds; placing signs in additional locations throughout your city; and using flag banners, such as those used at car dealerships.

Taking Calls

Once the signs are up, calls will start coming in—fast and numerous. Your number-one priority with every phone call is to commit the caller to coming to an open house. Your goal is to get potential clients to come to a showing, and to do so by giving out as little information as possible. Don't discuss financial information over the phone. This will confuse most callers, but more than this, it's impossible to give them hard numbers because of the flexibility of the program. Give them an opportunity to see the home and discuss the program with you in person.

Ideally, you'll hold two to three showings per week and have at least two people or parties at each showing. When you set up appointments, weekday evenings and Saturday afternoons are best. Do your best to schedule appointments with callers for no later than forty-eight hours after the call. If you're swamped with calls, call the first few back and tell them that the demand has been so high that you have had to move the showing up to the next evening.

Holding Your Open House

In June 2006, I experienced an ideal open house. I had closed on a property on a Monday, and it funded the next day. On Wednesday, I put out my signs and immediately started receiving calls. I got sick that day, so I decided to hold off on the open house. I didn't feel well enough until Saturday.

When I showed up Saturday morning, there were several people already waiting. As I walked into the home, I realized that I wouldn't be able to talk to everyone separately, so I asked them to take their time viewing the home, and then to come see me afterward. After ten minutes or so, I had about a dozen people huddled around me as I did a group presentation. I discussed the benefits of renting to own and went over all the financials. Three people filled out an application on the spot. After almost everyone had left, I hung back with the last couple. We spoke for thirty minutes, after which time they went to the bank to get enough money for an option consideration. My home was sold.

The best way to sell a rent-to-own contract is through an open house, for a few reasons. The first reason is efficiency. You can show the home once to several people, rather than setting up individual appointments. Another benefit is the natural pressure that is created from competition. When a showing includes multiple parties, everyone takes the qualification process more seriously and wants to be the first to qualify. Open houses are also the best way for you to explain the Compassionate Financing program with its flexible options.

The easiest way to explain the program is to have flyers prepared that show a few different scenarios, such as the following:

RENT 2 OWN

Stop Paying Rent!
Build Equity in a Short Period of Time.

[Property Address]
[Name of Person Taking Calls]
[Phone Number]

Compassionate Financing™ is often referred to as renting-to-own and is very different from paying rent. Its purpose is to help people stop throwing their money away on rent. Through this aggressive program, we will be crediting a very generous amount of your monthly payments towards the purchase price of the home so we can help you build thousands of dollars of equity by the end of the program. This allows you to build equity much faster than a bank would ever allow without the difficult qualification process. I am a very flexible and open-minded person to work with and I hope you realize that an investment opportunity like this is a rare find and I will be selective in whom I choose for this unique opportunity.

- You Can Make Any Improvements to the Home
- I Help You Improve Your Credit
- Build Thousands in Equity

Initial Down Payment	Total Monthly Payment	Equity Built Monthly	Total Equity Including $5000 Signing Bonus
$3,000	$1400	0	$8,000
$5,000	$1300	$100	$12,400
$7,000	$1200	$200	$16,800

Build your net worth and your retirement account by $8,000.00–$16,800.00 in the next 2 years!

Everything on the flyer is fairly self-explanatory until you get to the numbers. The first column of numbers shows three options for down payments. The key word for explaining these numbers is "flexible." Each situation is unique. Emphasize that you will work with the tenant you choose for the home. This is a selective process and you are *qualifying*, rather than selling them, on the home.

The down payment selected by the tenant then determines the monthly rent in the second column. Notice that the rent goes up if the tenant puts down less.

The third column shows the monthly equity portion the tenant will receive if he or she makes payments on time. On a small home with a traditional thirty-year mortgage, you may be lucky to get $50 per month credited toward principal, while the rest goes to interest. When we tell people that with our program they can build equity four times faster than they can with a bank, it's because we may credit them with up to $200 per month toward equity in the home—but *only* if they pay on time.

The fourth column has to do with bonus equity, which can be viewed as a signing bonus. This helps you provide one more incentive to someone who may be concerned about the condition of the home, or needs one more benefit to seal the deal. Many clients enter into our contracts with no bonus equity.

Qualifying Applicants

After a potential client looks at your flyer and makes it clear that he or she is interested, it's time to present him or her with an application. Since you're being the bank for your tenants, you need to act like a bank and qualify them well, though you're going to make it much easier for them than banks do.

Once you've received an application, it's time to decide whether the potential tenant qualifies or not. The following are the main criteria for making this decision:

- **Down Payment.** Can they afford the down payment? If they have money, it's because they are either resourceful or they've been saving, which are traits you're looking for in an applicant. If your potential client has almost no money and is trying to negotiate special long-term financing, then you run a much higher risk of eventual eviction. Our rule of thumb is to collect no less than $3,000 up front.

▶ **Monthly Payment.** Can they comfortably make the payment every month? Do not trust people to make this determination on their own. It is up to you to put yourself in their shoes and decide whether the payment is realistic. I like to ask these additional questions:

- Is their income based on commission? If so, have they performed consistently in the past? What evidence do you have of this?

- Do they receive additional income from other sources? How secure are those sources?

- What other financial obligations do they have? What other payments do they have (auto, recreational vehicles, child support, etc.)?

▶ **References.** Follow through and ask three of their references whether they pay on time, take care of their resources, and are financially dependable. If all their references are family members and friends, be sure to talk to at least a couple of nonbiased third parties, such as previous landlords.

▶ **Credit Report (Optional).** Sometimes there are benefits to pulling credit, but most of the time there are not. What do you expect to find on a credit report for a person who is trying to get seller financing on a home? There is obviously a reason why he or she cannot get conventional financing. The benefit of pulling credit is seeing what other financial obligations a person has. The application explains that by signing they give you permission to order and review their credit report. If you decide to do so, work with a loan officer at a brokerage that will charge you for the service and help interpret the report. Otherwise, you can visit websites that help you pull credit with proper authorization.

Once you feel comfortable with an applicant, set up an appointment to proceed in the process. Most Compassionate Financing contracts are sold after collecting three or four applications. After selecting an applicant, it's time to work out the terms and sign the contract.

Executing Contracts

Compassionate Financing requires two separate documents for your protection. The first contract is a simple Residential Lease Agreement, or rental contract. We also simultaneously use an Option Purchase Agreement, which specifies that your client is going to put money down and have the option in the future to buy the home. Using these two separate contracts helps protect you from a client ever claiming an "equitable interest" in the property. In other words, it makes it very clear that tenants do not own your properties, which limits your liability. If a tenant does not pay rent, it's fairly easy to get him or her out of the home. But if the tenant claims equitable interest, it's a much harder process.

> **Equitable Interest:** Interest held by virtue of an equitable title (a title that indicates a beneficial interest in property and that gives the holder the right to acquire formal legal title) or claimed on equitable grounds, such as the interest held by a trust beneficiary. (Source: *Black's Law Dictionary*).

In addition to using these two separate documents, be aware that we also use specific language to protect you from a client ever claiming that they have an equitable interest in the home. Consider the following:

- ▶ **Option Payment/Consideration:** This term is in reference to the down payment. We don't use the term "down payment," as it implies that the tenant put money into the home.

- **Accumulated Option Payment:** This term refers to the amount of money you credit to the client every month (only for on-time payments). This is similar to a bank's offer to apply part of your payment to principal when you are buying a home. Note that this is one of our finer sales points: We help our clients build equity faster than a traditional bank would allow them to by using this feature.

- **Credited Consideration:** This term refers to the bonus equity we sometimes offer clients to give them an extra incentive to sign the contract and get into the home. Although the contract has a blank space for this amount of money, it is never named in the contract specifically.

- **Liquidated Damage:** You will see this term in the Option Purchase Agreement. It means that any money the client puts down is nonrefundable, and the client cannot ever come back and ask for it back. It is not a penalty; it's simply a provision that says that your client cannot come back and ask for the money.

- **Credit/Equity:** These words imply an equitable interest in the home. If you see a derivation of these words in the contract, they are permitted in their context; otherwise you will not find this verbiage in the contracts.

- **Tenant/Landlord:** We do not use the terms "buyer" and "seller," as they also argue an equitable interest in the home.

Although we've spent years and thousands of dollars on attorneys perfecting our contracts, I'm providing them for free for readers of this book, since they're so critical to success on the Strait Path. Visit www.straitpathrealestate.com to download them now.

Dan, one of our investors, took his first property through this whole process last year. Having worked for years as a corporate trainer and critical-thinking consultant, Dan had been exposed to a lot of wealthy people. He realized that those who had made their money through a small business struggled through an intense three- to five-year period to make it through the founding stage, and most of them failed over time. On the other hand, of those that had made their money through real estate, only a small percentage failed and the rest were doing great. Because of these experiences, Dan had been interested in getting into real estate for a few years.

We met in late summer 2008, and he joined our program after researching REIC. With good credit, a solid income, and about $100,000 in liquid funds, he was ready to roll.

Within a couple of weeks of joining the program, he bought his first property with a purchase price of $182,000 and a market value of $230,000. Though the home had been cleaned immaculately, it was dated and located on a busy street, which actually made it an ideal home for the Strait Path system. Dan became a bit nervous about his investment when he started showing the home and the first few people provided negative feedback. However, he was encouraged upon receiving two to three phone calls per day from the first day he put out his signs.

After Dan had been advertising the property for about five weeks, a family told him they wanted the home. He made a mistake by taking down his signs before a contract was signed and he had received a down payment. This family ended up rescheduling three appointments, and then failed to show up for their final appointment and never returned future phone calls. They were apparently unable to find the down payment money.

Having learned a valuable lesson, Dan put up his signs again and started at square one. This time, within a month he had a solid family that had fallen in love with the home and were ecstatic about the program. One of their children had been born with a congenital heart disease, which forced them to accrue a mountain of medical bills and eventually declare bankruptcy. This had prevented them from buying a home a few years earlier. They had been living in an apartment, which was a terrible situation. Their downstairs neighbors were two drug users who would bang on doors and yell frequently. The couple was fearful of allowing their children to play in the play area. Though they had spoken with the landlord about the situation, he had refused to do anything about it.

Overjoyed with Compassionate Financing, they gladly put $5,000 down and are now paying $1,300 per month, of which $200 applies toward their eventual purchase. They have replaced the furnace and cleared the yard to install playground equipment, among other improvements. Dan receives a positive monthly cash flow of $200, and he never has to handle maintenance issues.

Compassionate Financing provides all of the benefits of rentals, flips, and lease options, while eliminating all of the flaws and pitfalls of each. With this program, you'll never have to fix a toilet again. You won't have to worry about how the market will perform. Most important, you'll feel great for providing a valuable service for individuals, families, and your community. You're getting people out of the rent trap and helping them increase their self-worth and wealth. You're providing options that are otherwise unavailable through traditional means.

And once you've gone through the process once, there's nothing stopping you from repeating it dozens of times to build long-term, sustainable wealth for your family.

Achieving Critical Mass

"Endurance is one of the most difficult disciplines, but it is to the one who endures that the final victory comes."

—Buddha

The Strait Path system is not for the inconsistent or impatient. It is not for the starry-eyed, spontaneous dreamers who skip from scheme to scheme. It is not a strategy to tinker with until you get bored or it becomes too hard. Rather, it is designed for disciplined, patient, and persistent investors with the wisdom to see into the future and the work ethic to make that future a reality.

The magic of the system manifests through plain repetition. Though it certainly enjoys revolutionary advantages, these are not substitutes for diligence. However, the beauty of Strait Path repetition is twofold: first, the system *is* actually replicable, which is much more than can be said of other short-lived strategies, and second, repetition creates exponential growth.

In this chapter you'll learn how to build wealth quickly and achieve critical mass on the Strait Path through discipline, speed, and leverage. Specifically, you'll learn the following principles and concepts:

- **The importance and power of delaying gratification.** This, combined with repetition, creates a "snowball" effect.

- **How to achieve exponential growth.** You've already learned how speed in the property-finding process differentiates Strait Path real estate. In this chapter you'll learn how speed elevates the system above others in a different way: the longer you stay on the path, the faster it gets.

- **How to leverage yourself and achieve infinite growth** through partnerships.

- **The power of collaboration.** You'll learn how to build a power team, which reduces your effort while increasing your profits. You'll also learn five forms of leverage and how they apply on the Strait Path.

DELAYING GRATIFICATION

I bought my first investment property when I was twenty-three years old. I had a friend at the time who was about my same age. We worked at the same place, made about the same amount of money, and were both able to qualify for about the same amount on a home mortgage.

I bought an older home well below a price that I could have actually qualified for. Furthermore, it had a mother-in-law apartment in the basement that I was able to rent out for $500 per month. This rental income brought my monthly mortgage payment from $800 down to $300 per month, which was $100 less than what I had been paying in rent. About six months later, I was able to refinance and get my mortgage down to $550, which meant that with the rental income I was really only paying $50 per month. The house was old, it needed some work, and it wasn't as big as my wife and I would have liked. But we had big goals that required short-term sacrifices.

Meanwhile, my friend bought a bigger and much nicer home. We later sold our investment home and made a $54,000 profit, and then moved on to many more investments, which have made us millions. Interestingly, my friend still lives in the same house and works the same job. I have nothing but love and respect for my friend. I'm not better than he or anyone else. I only bring up the story to illustrate the importance of delaying gratification.

"The single characteristic that rich people tend to have in common is an unusually long time horizon. In other words, rich people get rich because they think further ahead than the rest of us. As a matter of fact, research indicates that the length of your time horizon is the one characteristic that most accurately predicts where you will land in the socioeconomic strata . . . Wealthy people routinely plant seeds that won't bear fruit for months or even years."—Roy H. Williams, author, *Wizard of Ads* trilogy

---

Delaying gratification is the discipline aspect of achieving critical mass on the Strait Path. If you purchase only one or two properties and consume your initial profits by immediately increasing your lifestyle, you'll never make it to the end destination. You'll stray off the path, as if you were heading from California to Florida and but got waylaid in Las Vegas.

Having big dreams and goals usually requires that you shrink your standard of living for a while in order to achieve them. My advice is to reinvest 100 percent of your profits in the first few years of investing to build a solid foundation before you increase your expenditures and lifestyle. Doing so helps you create that chain reaction, or "snowball" effect, that is otherwise almost impossible to achieve. In fact, it comes down to the very definition of *leverage*, which essentially means to create a large output with relatively little input. It's an amplification process wherein your existing assets are amplified and magnified, thus growing into many more assets. Without delayed gratification, this power is severely restricted, if not eliminated.

What short-term price are you willing to pay for the sake of your greater dreams? Don't let today's wants get in the way of tomorrow's dreams. It takes nine months for a human baby to fully develop, which is called the gestational period. Likewise, all human achievements have a "gestational period." The fruits of achievement can never be greater than the roots of preparation and persistence.

"Everything that is great in life is the product of slow growth; the newer, and greater, and higher, and nobler the work, the slower is its growth, the surer is its lasting success. Mushrooms attain their full power in a night; oaks require decades. A fad lives its life in a few weeks; a philosophy lives through generations and centuries."—William George Jordan, author, *The Power of Truth*

Committing to the Strait Path system often requires accepting a new financial paradigm. This can be an exciting time when you envision a world of new possibilities. That excitement, however, must be balanced by discipline, which is why I stress sticking to a budget. Rethink all of your expenses and commit to saving as much as possible. If you can make a two-year commitment to save your money, and learn to prefer investing to spending, you will find that both your short-term spending funds *and* your long-term investments take flight.

In his classic book *The Richest Man in Babylon*, George Clason recommends saving 10 percent of everything you make in order to begin feeling more financial peace and to prepare for investing. Pay yourself before paying creditors and buying toys. Over time, as you become financially successful, make sure that it is not you but your money that is hard at work every day.

My friends and clients Rory and Andrea are well on their way to retirement because they have implemented the principle of delaying gratification. Rory works for a software company, and Andrea is a stay-at-home mother, as well as a part-time tax preparer. Knowing that they didn't want to be stuck in the W-2 employee trap all their lives and wanting to create passive income, they began looking for suitable investments. After conducting a diligent search and investigating several companies and investment options, they attended one of my seminars. After doing more research and meeting with me, they decided to move forward.

They lived in a single-family home and already owned a duplex, both of which had equity. Although they could have moved into a nicer home, they extracted their equity to purchase another investment property. They then moved into one of their duplex units while collecting rent from the other unit. Using Compassionate Financing, they found a tenant for the home they had just moved out of within one week. Their current cash flow covers all of their mortgages. Rather than buying extravagant things and living a high-consumption lifestyle, they're saving as much money as possible. They drive a sixteen-year-old car and are working on purchasing another investment home. Their goal is to have their investments pay for their consumption, which they know can be achieved within a relatively short period of time if they are willing to sacrifice now.

Delaying immediate gratification is the catalyst that accelerates the actualization of our ultimate dreams. It transfers energy that would have been wasted on frivolous things to things of greater importance. It is the key that unlocks the door to exponential and infinite growth on the Strait Path.

EXPONENTIAL GROWTH

In *The Tipping Point*, Malcolm Gladwell poses the puzzle of what happens when you fold a paper, fold it again, and continue folding it until you have refolded the paper fifty times. Most people, writes Gladwell, would "guess that the pile would be as thick as a phone book or, if they're really courageous, they'll say that it would be as tall as a refrigerator. But the real answer is that the height of the stack would approximate the distance to the sun. And if you folded it over one more time, the stack would be as high as the distance to the sun and back. This is an example of what in mathematics is called a geometric progression."

Investors enjoy a similar progression on the Strait Path. As you repeat the process over time, a whole new world opens up to you. Since you're amassing increasingly greater net worth and building higher cash flow, you're able to get approved for more and more homes. It creates a self-reinforcing cycle. This is especially true when you're managing your business properly and leveraging your LLCs. With proper seasoning and management, your business entities can purchase properties, rather than you having to use your personal credit.

Most real estate investors, however, piece together *ad hoc* strategies that change frequently based on new interests or on market conditions. As a result, they usually wash out of real estate investing entirely over time. But the only reason to change your strategy is if it's not working. I have a friend whose father has owned dozens of investment properties throughout his lifetime. Unfortunately, when his properties appreciated, he tended to use the equity for one expediency or another. And he soon grew tired of managing rentals that never provided adequate cash flow. He has since liquidated all of his properties and now has very little to show for his efforts.

The Strait Path system is the answer to this common scenario. Once you're on the path, there's absolutely no need to ever get off. If you're driving from Los Angeles to Miami, you don't stop in Texas and call it good. Likewise, neither can you succeed with this system if you purchase a couple of properties and then stop. Only through repetition will you reach your destination, which, in general terms, is achieving your ten-year retirement plan.

"Press on; nothing in the world can take the place of perseverance. Talent will not; nothing is more common than unsuccessful men with talent. Genius will not; unrewarded genius is almost a proverb. Education will not; the world is full of educated derelicts. Persistence and determination alone are omnipotent."—Calvin Coolidge, thirtieth president of the United States

Here's how it works practically: You purchase a discount property and then lease it through Compassionate Financing. Then, you either refinance the home as soon as possible or your tenant purchases the home (or both). Your profits are then used to purchase two more homes. Repeating the process with these two properties results in four homes, and so on. Our standard ten-year plan results in a net worth of more than $2 million and a passive six-figure income, though it all depends on how aggressive you want to be. In my case, I bought one home my first year of investing, the next year I bought two more, and the year after that I bought twelve more, for a total of fifteen after my third year. The next year I started using partnerships and subsequently purchased fifty homes; I purchased over one hundred homes in the year after that.

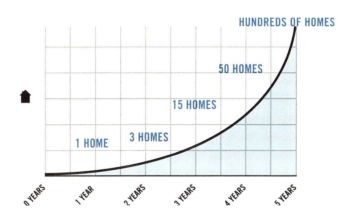

My good friend, business partner, and the CEO of Real Estate Investment Companies, Steve Earl, has enjoyed the benefits of exponential

growth. Steve has been a small business owner for many years. Before we met, he owned and operated a multimillion-dollar painting contracting business. About five years ago, he sold the business because he wanted to get into real estate.

He started by flipping. He purchased his first home and put $22,000 of material and labor into it. When he was done, the home was gorgeous. The problem was that he only made a $65 profit after selling it. He tried to sell it on his own for a while but was eventually forced to list it, which meant that his realtor received a fat check for $12,000, and Steve walked away with essentially nothing for his effort. However, he loved the process, so he continued flipping. He made a little bit of money, and on his sixth or seventh flip, he decided to get his real estate license so he could make a commission when he sold his homes. Predictably, he gravitated away from flipping as being a realtor became a full-time job.

As a realtor, his main interest was in buying, rather than selling, so he became extremely proficient at finding undervalued properties. In fact, Steve is the first realtor I ever encountered that could duplicate the finding results I was looking for. He helped me find one of my first homes, and we started working together. He was finding so many great deals that he couldn't handle them all. Since I couldn't handle them all either, I started bringing other people into my system. Steve became our exclusive realtor, and this relationship lasted for about a year and a half. After I started REIC, Steve came in and started our in-house property brokerage, the Real Estate Firm, and eventually helped me create a much bigger business.

Steve had done a lot of real estate prior to using the Strait Path system. After about seven years of intensive and broad experience, he concluded that Strait Path was the best system available, and he started working the system in his personal investing. His first Strait Path home was purchased for $210,000, and at an 18 percent discount he had $45,000 of equity. He has literally set foot on the property twice in his life, the first time being when he did a walk-through inspection, and the second time to show it to a tenant. In fact, he had a tenant before he had even closed on the property. He collected $6,000 down from his tenant and received a monthly positive cash flow of $500. Two years later, the tenant bought the home and Steve received $45,000 cash from the equity. Interestingly, as good of a deal as that was, he actually left another $35,000 on the table because he didn't use our recommended flexible purchase price in his contract. He had locked in the price and the home appreciated substantially.

Still, Steve was ecstatic about the results and promptly purchased another home from his proceeds. An estate sale, this home was worth $285,000 at the time, and Steve bought it for $215,000. He received a $4,500 option payment from one tenant, who unfortunately left due to a job transfer. His second tenant paid $5,000 down and is on track to purchase the home. An ideal tenant, he attends all of our classes, which are helping him repair his credit and prepare for purchasing the home. Steve was sold on him as a tenant when he walked through the home and announced, "I am going to live in this home until the day I die." Steve cash flows $250 per month on this property.

Since then, Steve has purchased two more properties using the Strait Path system, both of which are doing phenomenally well. Steve's goal is to sell his homes every two years and roll the proceeds into new properties. Within a few years, he will likely have ten properties paid for, which will generate about $15,000 of monthly cash flow.

Steve approaches real estate investing with the perspective of a lifelong business owner. He has been astounded at the comparison. Most small business owners work forty to sixty hours a week and are lucky to make $5,000 to $10,000 per month. Furthermore, very few businesses can be sold, and those that can be sold cannot profit enough to replace the income. In contrast, if all a person ever does on the Strait Path is own four homes free and clear after working the system for ten years—which is a very conservative plan—he or she will have over $1 million in salable assets that cash flow between $5,000 and $7,000 per month. Even more remarkable is the fact that this can be done by working about five hours per month. It gets even more incredible, however, when you factor in the tax benefits. Through 1031 exchanges (an IRS designation), investors can defer all capital gains taxes as they build their portfolios. In other words, if you purchase a property that appreciates by $50,000 in a few years, you can sell that property and purchase another without incurring taxes.

Where else are you able to find all of these benefits in one package? The exponential growth possibilities created by Strait Path real estate are unmatched.

INFINITE GROWTH

Suppose I put $40,000 down on a home worth $200,000, and the home produces an average annual return of 50 percent. After six months I refinance the home and get my principal back, and the home continues producing 50 percent annual returns. At that point—when the investment is generating a return with none of my own money in it—what is my actual return? Fifty percent, right? Wrong. My return is infinite; it's incalculable. If you put zero dollars into an investment, no matter how much you extract, your return is infinite. What other investment allows you to extract your initial investment and still produce the same returns in such a short period of time?

Strait Path real estate starts getting incredibly fun when you're able to generate infinite returns. This is achieved through partnerships. You can team up with family and friends to purchase far more properties than you can alone. You provide the knowledge and experience, and they provide their money and credit.

> **Calculate Your Ten-Year Game Plan on the Strait Path**
> To make the exponential growth possibilities of the system more real to you, visit www.straitpathrealestate.com and use our investment calculator to determine how much money you can make within ten years on the Strait Path.

Approach this with an attitude of service, rather than one of exploitation. Think of how you can help others by bringing this opportunity to them, rather than how much money you're going to make with them.

The more you succeed, the more others will want to know what you're doing and get involved. In fact, this is exactly how Real Estate Investment Companies was born—I had so many people asking me what I was doing that I realized I needed to magnify my efforts. Don't be surprised if complete strangers start approaching you, because they will. When you're ready to start partnering, you'll probably discover that you don't even need to market the opportunity—people will be lining up to pick your brain and profit from your success.

My good friend Rodney has had excellent success with partnerships. He and I grew up together and even attended the same college. While in college, he knew that I was doing real estate but was pretty skeptical. His dad had been self-employed his whole life and never had the security and success that Rodney wanted; Rodney wanted a "secure" career. After graduating with a business information technology degree, he took a job in Seattle. After a year of that, he realized that it wasn't going to get him where he wanted to go, so he started doing some soul-searching, which brought about some changes in his mind-set.

He called me ready to get into real estate investing. He eventually moved to Utah so I could train and help him. He quickly purchased his first investment, which he moved into. Since he was single, he rented out the other rooms and made enough to pay for the mortgage. He got so excited about the system that he began telling everyone he knew about it. Soon he was bringing in a lot of people to our events and workshops, and three of them wanted to partner with him. So far he has purchased homes with two of them, using their income and credit and his knowledge and effort, and he has formed an LLC with the third and they will be purchasing a home soon. His own investments jumped his net worth from −$33,000 to over $100,000, and his partnerships boosted his net worth to over $200,000.

Trent is another client who has leveraged partnerships. A builder by trade, he had finished a home just when the market was going down and thus wanted to sell quickly. He found a couple who wanted the home, but they couldn't buy it until theirs sold. They ended up swapping homes. He tried to sell the new home for ten months, but with no success. Then, he found out about our system, became a client, and used our system to sell the home within a month.

Like Rodney, he got excited about the system and began telling his family and friends about it. He partnered with his parents to purchase a home with $80,000 of equity and a positive monthly cash flow of over $500. He's also partnering with his father-in-law, and they will purchase a property together soon.

Infinite returns are generated on the Strait Path through leverage. As you leverage equity to refinance homes, you receive your invested principal back, and your homes continue generating income without your having your own money tied up in them. Also, by leveraging the cash and credit of partners, you can generate income without using your own money.

THE POWER OF COLLABORATION

"I'm not the smartest, but I surround myself with competent people."—Henry Ford, founder of Ford Motor Company

Another key principle of achieving critical mass on the Strait Path is collaboration. People often ask how I've been able to build such a successful organization at such a young age. The answer to that question lies in this section.

I learned so many positive lessons from my father that it would take a book to describe them. However, I also learned from his example how not to do one thing in particular, which has made all the difference in my career. He was a hardworking immigrant, a master craftsman from Germany. As I grew up, he was self-employed doing remodeling work. During long summers in my youth, he put me to work with his employees, and sometimes it was just he and I on projects.

Because of his reputation, he had access to plenty of work. Unfortunately, I watched him turn down job after job. I would often ask why he didn't expand his business, and his reply was always the same: "If you want something done right, do it yourself." He didn't trust others to work the tools with the accuracy and skill that he possessed. However, he could have expanded his business and been more profitable.

While I came to admire his beautiful craftsmanship and personal integrity, I have learned to train and delegate in order to expand. I created specialists to perform specific parts of my system. I was willing to give up a portion of profits to have team members help me do real estate more successfully than I was able to do alone. As Henry Ford exemplified, I realized that I needed to get the right people on board and become a good delegator.

Here's my "secret": *I have learned that if you really want something done right, do not do it yourself.* If you assemble the right power team and collaborate, you will find that you give up a small part of the profits only to do much less of the work. This is one critical way to achieve massive leverage in your investing efforts. Leverage, of course, means to produce substantial results with relatively little effort. There are five forms of leveraging, which include the following:

- Other People's Money
- Other People's Time/Labor
- Other People's Experience/Knowledge
- Other People's Ideas
- Other People's Systems

After I had purchased twenty-five investment properties and had a positive cash flow of more than $10,000 per month, I realized I needed to expand my abilities through leverage. I began hiring people to help with certain tasks and gave up 10 percent of the profits to eliminate almost 100 percent of the work. I first hired a couple of people to find deals. I asked sellers to pay for my loan fees, which meant that I could outsource loans without paying for them. I then hired others to sell my lease options for me, as well as to handle property management.

These initial efforts have grown into almost a dozen businesses. I followed Michael Gerber's advice, found in his excellent book *The E-Myth Revisited*. My businesses aren't dependent on me to make every decision; I find the best people, build systems, and empower people to make decisions.

Building a Power Team

Those who burn out in real estate try to do too much by themselves. If you're trying to do everything, not only are you going to burn out, but you're also going to make mistakes along the way. Everyone has different talents, interests, and insights that can be drawn upon. Real estate is a highly technical industry with a lot of moving parts. It's like a living organism, always changing and evolving. Staying up-to-date on every aspect is a commitment that few can keep—even for those people for whom real estate is their core passion. Even if you eat, drink, and breathe real estate, successful real estate investing requires a team of experts—what I call a "power team"—that you can count on to spread the workload around. I recommend that you fill at least the following roles on your real estate–investing power team:

- Realtor
- Mortgage broker
- Title officer
- Certified public accountant
- Attorney
- Banker
- Insurance broker

These individuals and others will do most of the legwork for you, if you form the right relationships through training. You'll leverage your Strait Path knowledge, experience, ideas, and system, and leverage their time, effort, and money. Your time and effort will thus be significantly reduced, but your results will improve exponentially. This is the power of collaboration.

On an even deeper level, Real Estate Investment Companies is the ultimate power team. Our team performs over 90 percent of the work for our investors. The program first started as my personal power team, but they were so good at handling my real estate demands that I expanded the group into a power team large enough to assist others with building their portfolios.

Strait Path real estate is much more than a real estate strategy; it's a holistic mind-set and a complete system for replacing America's flawed financial paradigm and escaping the traps of accumulation. When understood in this comprehensive context, it's easy to see why it's so important to stay the course. Buying one house will do great things for your financial situation; sticking with the system until you have purchased ten or more will thoroughly transform your life. Strait Path isn't about supplementing your income with a few hundred dollars a month; it's about creating a legitimate opportunity for retirement and higher purpose.

> **Learn How to Form a Power Team**
>
> Visit www.straitpathrealestate.com to learn how you can create your own power team, or take advantage of REIC's in-house power team.

Financial Liberation: Moving from Mechanics to Meaning

"Don't make money your goal. Instead, pursue the things you love doing, and then do them so well that people can't take their eyes off you."

—Maya Angelou

I want to start this chapter with two potentially shocking statements. First, the core of this book is not about real estate. Second, if your goal is to make money through real estate, you're self-deceived. I don't mean to offend; I simply mean to jolt you out of real estate mode so that we can move to higher, deeper, more important things, and to make some critical points.

Would it surprise you to learn that real estate is not my core passion? I know how strange that must sound coming from a person who has built a career on real estate investing. What I truly love about real estate is its ability to fund my deeper, more meaningful passions. To me, it's a tool I use to perform my real function in life; it's a means to an end. The true end for me is to experience personal freedom, to cultivate and share my highest gifts, and to help others do the same.

My passion is to help others unleash their natural abilities and their own passions. I discovered deeper joy through real estate by watching my clients succeed than by experiencing success myself. I revel in building businesses and systems that support financial liberation in all those I reach. I love extracting people from the 71 percent of all people who aren't happy with their work and helping them discover and live "Soul Purpose," a term I learned from Steve D'Annunzio (see www.soulpurposeinstitute.com). You may have heard this referred to as a "mission" or "higher calling." Though I no longer have to continue working, I see too many people who can benefit from the Strait Path system, and that's what drives me onward.

My hunch is that very few people are passionate about real estate for the sake of real estate. It's only an end for a very small minority. For the rest of us, it's simply a means to an end. We have different goals and dreams that we want to fulfill other than just buying a few investment properties. The fact is that these goals and dreams require money. And real estate is perhaps the single best tool for generating significant wealth in a relatively short time period for most individuals.

Having said that, understand that if there is just one thing I could teach my readers, it's this: *Financial liberation has nothing to do with money.* Financial liberation means maintaining a mind-set of abundance regardless of one's financial state and material possessions. It is a state of mind, an attitude, an ongoing commitment to replace fear, doubt, and worry with faith, love, and wisdom.

Just as real estate investing is a means to an end, nobody actually wants money itself. We want things that money will buy (or at least that we think it will buy), such as security, comfort, recreation, status, luxury, impact, and fame. But what we really want—though often this desire is subconscious—is financial liberation. Financial liberation means identifying your most worthy goals and then pursuing them, regardless of what's in your bank account. It means that your entire pursuit of money revolves around your higher ideals; it means to transcend the self-deception of pursuing money for the sake of money. It means giving yourself permission to go after your ideal life without waiting for that ever illusive "someday." It's about becoming the best version of you. It's about manifesting your innermost passions and gifts in profound service to the world. It's about fulfilling your highest aspirations.

"I know of no more encouraging fact than the unquestioned ability of a man to elevate his life by conscious endeavor."
—Henry David Thoreau, author, *Walden*

CONTENT VS. CONTEXT

Strait Path real estate provides the mechanics of wealth creation. While this is valuable, it is dangerously incomplete. Like power, material wealth for its own sake corrupts the individual who acquires it. When it is a person's highest goal, then that person's life is an empty shell of what he is actually capable of.

There is a profound difference between content and context. In the absence of context, all content is meaningless. For example, are bricks good or bad? Bricks are content; we need context to answer the question. If I use a brick to hit someone in the head, that's a bad use of bricks. On the other hand, if I use them to build a homeless shelter, this is arguably a good use of bricks.

Wealth and the means of acquiring wealth are content. The *context* is the meaning, the motivation behind them. Suppose a reader of this book applies Strait Path real estate to acquire $3 million in ten years. Is that a good thing? What if that reader uses the money to fund terrorism? What if he or she allows it to drive a life of complacency and subsequent moral degeneration? I don't want to just teach people how to make money through real estate; if that were my sole intention, I would be doing people an awful disservice. After having become wealthy through real estate, I promise you that it's not about the money. It's not about the nice home or fancy car you can buy with the money. It's not about living a lavish lifestyle. Rather, it's about making a positive impact on the world, leaving a legacy that will be felt for generations.

Only when I help people move from the mechanics of wealth to the meaning behind wealth can I feel like I've created lasting value in the world. Most people are held captive by an "I'll serve when" mentality, as in, "I'll do good in the world when I have more money." "I'll pursue my real dreams when I have enough money to afford them." Sadly, only a tiny few ever follow through on such mind-sets and statements; after acquiring wealth, they forget their original "why." They put off more meaningful things until they've "caught up with the Joneses," and by this time they're so entrenched in that lifestyle that they don't even know it. The challenge is to discover and pursue your true meaning *before* applying wealth mechanics. Do this and you'll be head and shoulders above most people before you ever get started.

"You are not here merely to make a living. You are here to enable the world to live more amply, with greater vision, and with a finer spirit of hope and achievement. You are here to enrich the world. You impoverish yourself if you forget this errand."—Woodrow Wilson, twenty-eighth president of the United States

---

MYTHS AND FALLACIES THAT LIMIT FINANCIAL LIBERATION

Financial liberation is beyond most people's reach because of the following four myths and destructive mind-sets:

1. The Retirement Myth
2. The Financial Freedom Myth

3. The Entitlement Mentality

4. The Fallacy of "Someday"

The Retirement Myth

The retirement myth is the idea that the purpose of life is to work for thirty years, save enough money, and then stop working and live off one's savings. This destructive myth causes many people to stay in jobs they don't like and that don't allow them full expression of their best talents. It makes us sell our "birthright" for a "mess of pottage" in the form of golden handcuffs and benefits. It often leads to small lives built around limited dreams.

In contrast to this myth, the financially liberated find what they love to do, regardless of what it may cost them in short-term benefits and illusory security. If you're doing what you love, why would you ever want to retire? Why would you ever want to escape? How can one retire from living their core purpose? In this mind-set, life is a continuum, where new life phases only lead to higher contributions.

The Financial Freedom Myth

The core difference between those operating under this myth and those with the retirement mind-set is that these people are just a little more ambitious. They don't want to wait until they are sixty-five; they want to be free now. However, for most people, being financially free has very little to do with their highest purpose in life. It signifies freedom *from* having to work, without detailing the freedom *to* live and serve with more meaning. I associate it with the "playboy" lifestyle. As I've perceived it, it's based on materialism rather than meaning. It hinges on having money, rather than revolving around values and ideals.

But more than this, my issue with "financial freedom" is that it is indefinite and dependent upon externalities. When will you be financially "free"? When you are worth $1 million? When you have $3 million of liquid cash? When your house is paid off? Is there not an internal liberation that one can achieve in spite of such external circumstances? Is it possible to transcend time and account balances and be free regardless by living your higher purpose?

The Entitlement Mentality

I'm not alone in believing that Americans, through ease and plenty, have developed an entitlement mentality. We feel entitled to retirement, to comfort, to job security, to health care, to work benefits. This leads to wallowing in victimhood, rather than achieving victory. It leads to the relinquishing of personal responsibility and perceiving that other people owe us our desired lifestyle. Rather than proactively pursuing personal fulfillment, we wait around for other people and circumstances to fall into place. We wait for our "ship" to come in, rather than swimming out to meet it, or simply creating it.

The Fallacy of "Someday"

"Someday I'll own a business." "Someday I'll take a trip to Europe." "Someday I'll run for political office." "Someday I'll lose weight." You've heard these and other similar thoughts expressed, or perhaps you've even expressed them yourself, right? We all do. The problem is this: When is someday? There are certainly things that require planning and patience, but "someday" is but a counterfeit of such wisdom and perseverance. The lack of money is just a symptom of the lack of purpose in one's life; money cannot fill that void.

"Someday" is an excuse for playing small in the moment. If you really want something, then sit down and create a comprehensive plan for achieving it, complete with a timeline, detailed steps, and what you're willing to do. The financially liberated don't casually spout out "somedays"; they deliberately proclaim specifics.

FROM MECHANICS TO MEANING

So here's my question for you: What do you really want to be and do in the short time you have on this earth? Have you defined this clearly enough? Are you willing to sacrifice for it? Are you willing to transcend myths, fallacies, and limitations in its pursuit? Are you willing to become financially liberated and live for purpose and meaning beyond money, to maintain an attitude of abundance in the face of challenges and trials, to overcome scarcity in all its destructive forms?

If so, then go after that meaning—make it your true end, and relegate Strait Path real estate to its rightful place as the means to that end. What if you got your priorities straight now—before you became financially successful—rather than waiting, like most people do? How much pain and wasted time and energy would that save you? What if you set out to serve, having the faith that money would follow, rather than setting out to make money, with service as a faint afterthought? How much more would you impact the world and contribute to peace and happiness?

> "What you leave behind is not what is engraved in stone monuments, but what is woven into the lives of others."
> —Pericles, Greek statesman

I've always been impressed by Bill and Melinda Gates. Having amassed a fortune, they formed the "largest transparently operated charitable foundation in the world." The foundation improves the health of those in developing countries by "giving them the chance to lift themselves out of hunger and extreme poverty," and in the United States, the foundation seeks to "ensure that all people—especially those with the fewest resources—have access to the opportunities they need to succeed in school and life." In 2007, after giving more than $28 billion to charity, Bill and Melinda became the "second most generous philanthropists in America." What strikes me about this, however, is that *every* individual has the potential to play just as big of a role. Within each of us are dreams that are every bit as important as what Bill and Melinda have accomplished—most of us simply lack the funding to bring them to fruition.

If your primary focus is to accumulate more and more wealth, it will never be enough. You will never reach a point of fulfillment. There will never be a turning point from selfish accumulation to service-based utilization. You can never accumulate enough of what you don't need because *what you don't need can never satisfy you*. But when you choose financial liberation, you'll always feel fulfilled.

"Balance, peace, and joy are the fruit of a successful life. It starts with recognizing your talents and finding ways to serve others by using them."—Thomas Kinkade, painter

---

REIC investors Carl and Cindy are stellar examples of people who want wealth for all the right reasons. Carl works in a manufacturing plant and Cindy is a mother with a drive to help the needy. Having been raised by parents who instilled within them a love of service, helping others is a natural and integral part of their lives. A few years ago—long before they began applying Strait Path real estate—Cindy started a program where she collects leftover food from the local school districts and distributes it to homeless shelters, battered women's shelters, and other charitable organizations. Over time Cindy's program has grown into a large operation as bakeries and other food providers have begun donating food. Wanting to continue the legacy of service that was taught to them, they have included their children in all these efforts. The children help Cindy prepare food and make deliveries. But Carl and Cindy have much bigger dreams beyond this operation, which their investments are beginning to fuel and fund. Eventually, they want to be involved with or start their own global charitable organizations. They have no desire for a luxury lifestyle; they simply want enough to provide a comfortable life for their family and then use the rest to fund meaningful philanthropy.

I challenge you to become financially liberated now, today, immediately. It's an internal choice, not an external event. It's a commitment to becoming who we were meant to become. It is to live a life of inspiration and dedication, to hold as sacred your life, your choices, and your potential. This is opposed to the stagnant life, which holds no new exciting truths and where we are simply left to the waves of life, tossed about whichever way the sea may take us.

"Destiny is not a matter of chance, it is a matter of choice; it is not a thing to be waited for, it is a thing to be achieved."
—William Jennings Bryan, U.S. secretary of state under Woodrow Wilson

---

FINDING AND LIVING MEANING THROUGH WISE STEWARDSHIP

Financial liberation is best achieved by understanding that our lives, gifts, and resources are our stewardship. We are caring for something that is not our own. We tend to take better care of things that belong to others than we do of the things that belong to us. We enter this life with no material resources, and we leave with nothing. Everything we're blessed with during our lives is a gift to be utilized wisely and unselfishly. Those who understand money as an entrustment and live accordingly receive more. The wealth of those who spend carelessly and hoard selfishly is diminished. We are trusted with more material prosperity when we demonstrate that we're able to handle it.

Material accumulation can become a sickness. In the name of "security" or recreation, we can accumulate so much that our possessions actually possess us. The wise steward is a utilizer, not an accumulator. Steward-investors understand that there are much bigger purposes than earning money for purely selfish reasons. This understanding gives depth, context, and passion to their investing. It infuses them with meaning and motivation.

Such investors are also charitable. Whether you call it charity, tithing, or karma, it's a universal teaching that when we serve others and give of ourselves, we always get paid back in multiple blessings. While I'm not qualified to tell you what you should do with your money, I have found charity to be a true principle, and I invite you to consider it. My experience is that most people already practice charity anyway, so I doubt I'm introducing anything new to you. It's really just common sense. Our service facilitates joy in others and makes the world a better place. Everyone benefits when love and service are extended—including and especially those on the giving end.

Charity is at the heart of the sustainability issue that I frequently raise. So many investment strategies and systems fail because they fail to serve. If an investment does not make the world a better place, it will always fail. In this sense, the service is not an afterthought, but rather the primary intention of abundance-minded individuals and successful investors. I encourage you to be generous and discover the best motivation for accumulating wealth.

Be charitable where you have received; follow the concept "pay it forward." If someone has been kind to you, forward it by being kind to others. If a mentor teaches you a life-altering principle, then be a mentor for someone in need. If Strait Path real estate eliminates your retirement worries and transforms your financial life to one of abundance, then share it with others. Giving can be done in the form of sharing our time, talents, and finances. All of these make great gifts of service.

In the end, we should be seeking to better our families and those around us. When we have the intention of taking care of more than our own needs, life seems to arrange itself to take care of us as well. As I've learned from author and life coach Steve D'Annunzio, life isn't a game of chess, where we're trying to outmaneuver and outsmart others to our gain and their detriment. We're not here to play a win-lose game. No person's gifts are any more important or valuable than another's. We're all connected, and everyone wins when we use our gifts to lift one another.

Stewardship applies to much more than material prosperity. It extends to our thoughts, actions, habits, and beliefs. It encompasses our physical, mental, spiritual, and emotional well-being. Everything we do matters. Every thought and every act carries a consequence, all of which compound over time. The person you become in twenty years from now will be the result of what you do today and tomorrow. Small things repeated become big accomplishments—or big failures.

"The person determined to achieve maximum success learns the principle that progress is made one step at a time. A house is built one brick at a time. Football games are won a play at a time. A department store grows bigger one customer at a time. Every big accomplishment is a series of little accomplishments."—David Joseph Schwartz, professor

---

Wise stewardship helps you build the life that you really want, which is a reflection of your core values and aspirations. Author and speaker Brian Tracy has a great success principle called "Everything counts." Everything we do adds to, or detracts from, our life and goals. Stop and consider your actions and where you are headed. You may be surprised to discover that many of your daily actions are actually counterproductive and keep you from achieving your own goals. Evaluate your actions and retain the ones that keep you on the path, and drop the ones that don't, because everything does, indeed, count.

"Everything counts. No efforts are ever lost. Every extraordinary accomplishment is the result of thousands of ordinary accomplishments that no one recognizes or appreciates. The greatest challenge of all is for you to concentrate your thinking single-mindedly on your goal and by the law of attraction, you will, you must, inevitably draw into your life the people, circumstances, and opportunities you need to achieve your goals."—Brian Tracy, author

---

My friend Tony has exemplified this principle perfectly. He was raised to think that being wealthy was the result of lying, cheating, stealing, or luck. He was taught that lifelong financial struggle was the price of being honest. He was resigned to the struggle until he saw a few key people in his life succeeding financially and doing the things that he really wanted to do. Seeing that set a mental shift in motion for him.

He began interviewing everyone he could find who was either wealthy or headed in the direction he wanted to go to learn how they thought, what they did, and what their habits were. One of these people taught him to fill his mind with good information. Tony bought an iPod and downloaded an entire library of audio books, full of great titles on self-improvement and wealth creation. Tony began listening to these books everywhere he went—walking to school, driving in the car, and every other opportunity he could find, totaling an hour or two every day. Over time it added up to hundreds of hours of the education he needed to overcome his previous mind-set. He felt as if a whole new world of possibilities had opened to him.

He developed a passion for helping others learn and apply the same knowledge. He was frustrated with companies who provided education without hands-on implementation, so he started looking for a place where he could help people with both. He came across Real Estate Investment Companies, and he loved the system and asked how he could work with us. He was twenty-two years old, an unemployed full-time student and newlywed, and he had no current means of investing. However, because of his educational habit, he had the drive and will to succeed. He began educating himself and started working with us on a commission basis. He also started preparing to invest and has since closed his first investment deal. By the time he is twenty-four years old, he'll have at least two investment properties.

Tony is now in the exact position he had envisioned—teaching people wealth and success principles, and helping them apply them practically. With no experience and very little formal education in his field, he now makes as much as an average MBA graduate—and he's still attending college. He credits the bulk of his current success to his commitment to learn something new every day. A small habit that began with a desire and an iPod has flourished into a full-time, successful, and fulfilling career.

Travis is another of my friends who has realized that everything counts. He joined our program a couple of years ago and has purchased two homes using the Strait Path system. Everything has gone fairly well for him except for a minor struggle within the last few months. He was having difficulty getting a tenant for one of his homes. After the home had been vacant for four months, it started to consume his thoughts, dragging him down into worry and negativity.

With some encouragement from a few friends, Travis purchased several books and audio CDs and began inputting the right information into his brain to counteract his negative thoughts. This led him to realize that he hadn't done as much as he could and should have done to get a tenant. He had become casual in running the system. For example, he hadn't been showing the property to tenants and was mostly answering questions over the phone, which we've learned is ineffective. Because he was working on changing his outlook, he started focusing more on the things he could control and less on the things over which he had no control. He analyzed where he was going wrong and recommitted to running the system properly.

Within weeks of starting to read and refocus, he received calls from two excellent prospective tenants who were excited about his home. After putting $3,000 down, one of them is now renting Travis's home for $1,400 per month.

Wise stewards are vigilant about how they spend their time, what they put into their minds and bodies, the words they say, and the habits they cultivate. They are highly conscientious of the little things that they know become big things over time. Stewardship is essential to successful investing and, ultimately, financial liberation.

Financial liberation isn't about accumulating money for oneself. It's about becoming who you were born to become and serving as many people as possible. It's about making the world better, more peaceful, and more prosperous. It's about overcoming obstacles and transcending fear and greed. It's about creating value and solving problems. It's about stopping the madness of institutional dependence and becoming self-reliant and more productive with our resources.

Anyone can read this book, apply Strait Path real estate, and become wealthy safely and in a relatively short period of time. But the true message behind the system is that it can empower you to fully live your dreams and manifest your passions, and not for selfish reasons. It can equip you with the tools and resources to live your Soul Purpose, which can have profound impact on the world.

The lesson I hope you'll learn is that it's not about the money—it's about what you can do with the money. Money is value neutral. It is the mind-sets and actions of people that give it value. It's been said many times—and it's absolutely true—that if you're selfish now, more money will only make you more selfish. If you're wise, charitable, and aligned with true principles now, more money will make you better able to serve.

I invite you to become an investor of depth, substance, and wisdom. I invite you to choose financial liberation. If you properly apply Strait Path real estate, it's inevitable that you'll become wealthy. That's no longer in question—your wealth is assured. The deeper, more important question is what you will do with your wealth and who you will become in the process.

My real passion behind real estate is the possibility it creates to improve the world by enabling thousands of people to live the most meaningful life possible. You're not going to achieve this using the standard and flawed retirement mind-set. You have very little assurance that mutual funds, IRAs, and 401(k)s will create the lifestyle and financial security you want. Identify the highest and noblest reasons to become wealthy, and then follow through with the Strait Path system with discipline and integrity. Work to achieve your ideals, not solely to make money. Be wise and self-reliant. Take control of your life and finances. Make a difference and leave a legacy.

The seed of greatness embedded in your soul is nothing short of holy. I know most of us feel this in our quiet, most intimate moments. And if more of us viewed our lives in this sacred light, how much pain and suffering would be alleviated and even eliminated? How much wiser would our daily choices be if we considered them in the context of this deeper, higher consciousness?

"Freedom is useless if we don't exercise it as characters making choices . . . We are free to change the stories by which we live. Because we are genuine characters, and not mere puppets, we can choose our defining stories. We can do so because we actively participate in the creation of our stories. We are coauthors as well as characters. Few things are so encouraging as the realization that things can be different and that we have a role in making them so."—Daniel Taylor, author, *The Myth of Certainty*

Why you choose real estate is, of course, your business. Still, I invite you to identify a greater, more authentic reason than making money and achieving financial security. Money is but a surface-level desire that conceals your real reasons for wanting it. Where do you fit into the grand scheme of things? Have you ever felt that you had a higher calling in life but were held back by feelings of inadequacy? Through real estate, you have an unprecedented opportunity to pause from life's demands and get in touch with what you really want to be, do, and have. Through real estate, you can fund noble projects and bring vision into reality. As you become financially liberated, you're empowered to leave a legacy that will be felt for generations.

When I started this chapter by declaring that this book is not about real estate, my point was that real estate is just a means to an end. My life is dedicated to helping you arrive at your true ends, and real estate is just a great vehicle for carrying you there. Our investment program helps you achieve more than just your financial goals. It helps you fulfill your Soul Purpose. I hope you'll use the vehicle of real estate, but more important, I hope you'll drive in the right direction. And the best and surest way to do this is to define your final destination *before* getting onto the path.

So what is *your* final destination, and how can I help you get there?

CONCLUSION

From "What If?" to "What Next?"

> "Two roads diverged in a wood, and I . . . I took the one less traveled by, and that has made all the difference."
>
> —**Robert Frost**

What if the claims I've made in this book are true? What if the stories from our clients are real? What if you could eliminate almost all of the risk of real estate and build wealth quickly and safely? What if it's possible for you, no matter your circumstances, to create millions of dollars through real estate in a few short years? What if what you're currently doing won't get you to where you want to go?

What if you had a crystal ball that showed you what your life would be like in five or ten years if you applied the Strait Path system—or if you didn't?

Of course, no one can see into the future, but hindsight is twenty-twenty. I've met thousands of people as a result of my real estate system, all of them with different past experiences and current circumstances. Some have applied my system to achieve phenomenal results. I've often wondered, "What would their lives be like if they had chosen a different route?" Others tell me, "Kris, if only I had met you a few years ago!" as they recount disappointing stories of financial loss. I'm struck by the same thought—what would their lives be like today if they had been introduced to Strait Path real estate sooner? How much pain and loss could have been avoided? How much would they have been able to produce and retain?

I don't want you to live your life with regret, nor should you compare yourself with others. However, if you've made financial mistakes in the past, it's important to learn from them to create a better, wiser future. And if you haven't made mistakes yet, you undoubtedly will unless you can learn from others. As the proverb goes, "Wise men learn by other men's mistakes, fools by their own." For those readers who have researched other real estate systems or have studied real estate but have never acted, this is your opportunity to make up for lost time. This is your chance to apply your knowledge, to remotivate yourself to do what it takes to reach your goals.

As you conclude this book and ponder your own financial future, I invite you to learn from the experiences of others—both good and bad—that I've included on my website. The purpose of sharing these stories is to create space for your mind to explore possibility. As you read the stories of loss and failure, read them with the abiding thought, "What would my life be like if I had learned about Strait Path real estate sooner?" And as you read the success stories, think, "What could my life be like if I apply this knowledge, starting now?"

Visit www.straitpathrealestate.com now to download and read these "what if" stories.

THE TRUE VALUE OF LOST OPPORTUNITY

Understanding your "what if" is immensely important, yet few people truly understand how deep it really goes. Suppose you lose $10,000 in a bad investment. Most people only see the $10,000 lost. But in such a case you've lost much more than that. What you've really lost is what that $10,000 *could have been* had it been invested more wisely. For example, what if you had invested that into Strait Path real estate? Assuming a 50 percent noncompounding average annual rate of return—which is much lower than our average client enjoys—$10,000 would have grown to $35,000 within five years, and that $35,000 would have turned into $122,500 within another five years.

Lost opportunity costs compound negatively just as interest compounds positively. Lost money is never the initial dollar amount lost—what you actually lose is what the money could have grown to. This dollar amount represents a painful "what if." Lost money, time, and productivity can never be regained. We can learn from those mistakes and move forward with more wisdom. However, the obvious ideal is to reduce lost opportunity costs as much as possible by finding sound and sustainable investment strategies and adhering to true principles.

So what is *your* "what if"? How would your life be different today had you applied the Strait Path system five years ago? Where could it be five or ten years from now if you start applying it today? Everyone has a "what if," but my passion is to turn those "what if's" and "if only's" into "what next," as in "Now that we've achieved financial independence, what's next?" The Strait Path system has a 0 percent failure rate. Literally every person who applies it properly succeeds and creates greater and safer wealth for themselves and their families.

Are you open to possibility? Can you begin thinking of the contribution you will make once you become independently wealthy? Do you want to live the "what if" life? Or do you want to embrace the "what next" life? Only you can make the choice, but once you do, the path is clear and straight, the obstacles have been eliminated for you, and the results are inevitable. Welcome to Strait Path real estate.

Acknowledgments

As a new husband with no investing track record, I purchased my first little house and started this amazing adventure. I felt so strongly about it that I got it under contract before even talking to my wife, Kalenn. I am so fortunate that she supported me after finding out about it, even though it was a nasty fixer-upper. She has done the same on every deal since, and I count myself among the happiest of men because Kalenn embraces my business passion so fully.

My parents, Klaus and Eileen, deserve so much praise. During my extraordinary childhood, they taught me the American dream and filled me with the confidence that I could achieve it.

I also want to thank Matt and Laurie King, my first business partners, who believed in me enough to buy dozens of homes with me.

I honor my dear friend Stephen Miller as the first member of the Real Estate Investment Companies power team, who made so many sacrifices to begin this incredible journey with me. Kevin Clayson, the second member of the team, remains one of the most influential members of the REIC team and an invaluable friend.

I also want to thank Steve Earl, my business partner, responsible for so much growth, structure, and improvement to the company. Steve is the best business partner I've ever had, and I look forward to a lifetime of friendship and success with him.

I extend profound gratitude to everyone who has supported me in life, in my real estate, the creation of REIC, and the production of this book, including Mike Krohn, Tyler Bennett, Stephanie Badders, Brett and Lynda Cherry, Tyler Bennett, Ruben Mena, Christopher Wood, Garrett White, Christine Graham, and everyone else on the REIC team.

I thank all of our investors for teaching us how to make REIC what is today.

Finally, this book would have been nearly impossible to produce without my good friend and writer Stephen Palmer. It was an honor to work with Stephen because of his writing style and experience, as well as his personal knowledge of and experience with real estate investing.

APPENDIXES

APPENDIX A

How to Join the REIC Program and Get on the Strait Path

To learn more about how REIC can help you build a real estate portfolio, visit www.reicglobal.com. You'll find detailed information on the investment program, the benefits we offer, the experiences of our investors, and how to sign up. This is not an educational program, where you're paying for education alone. We do offer education, but in contrast to other programs and systems, the purpose of the REIC investment program is to help you actually invest in real estate.

The best place to start is to attend one of our live seminars, or view a recorded seminar on our website.

After attending or viewing a seminar, you can complete our brief application, which helps us understand your situation. We'll then set up a phone call to answer your questions and cover specifics. From there we'll help you create a personalized ten-year game plan and show you exactly how to implement it. If this plan resonates with you, you'll pay the initial fee and get assigned a personal coach who will contact you within a few days to guide you through the process.

Finally, we plug you into the process, help you buy your first home, and set you soundly on the Strait Path. Our average investor buys a home within the first three months of joining the program.

Start now at www.reicglobal.com.

APPENDIX

Bonus Downloads and Resources

The following supplemental resources can be found for free at www.straitpathrealestate.com.

- **Investment Comparison Calculator.** Calculate where you'll be ten years from now following the traditional retirement plan versus the Strait Path.

- **Download: How to Execute Creative Real Estate Investing.** This is a valuable resource for anyone with underdeveloped or poor credit. It teaches you how to get started immediately on the Strait Path without having to qualify for loans.

- **Download: Fix vs. Don't Fix.** This download provides detailed guidelines on how to make wise decisions about worn and outdated homes. It shows what things you should spend money fixing versus home repair issues to avoid in order to reduce your risk.

- **Video: How to Perform a Comprehensive Market Analysis.** This video walks you through the market analysis process with precise detail. It helps you avoid mistakes when purchasing investments and teaches how to substantiate your equity position.

- **Mortgage Prequalification Process.** Our partner company, Strategic Lending, will show you how much real estate you qualify for right now. You'll find details on the website.

- **Download: Compassionate Financing Contracts Package.** We've spent thousands of dollars on attorneys and worked hundreds of hours perfecting our contracts to limit risk and liability. We've made both of our contracts—the rental contract and the Option Purchase Agreement—available to readers of this book, along with a document that explains each.

- **Video: Learn How to Form a Power Team.** Learn how you can create your own power team, or take advantage of REIC's in-house power team.

- **Webinar: Financial Liberation.** On this recorded webinar I explore the concept of financial liberation in greater detail in order to empower you in your financial and life decisions.

- **"What If" Case Studies.** These real-life examples illustrate—for better or worse—the true value of lost opportunity costs. The stories of financial loss point out where people would be today had they learned about the Strait Path sooner, and the success stories illustrate the positive effects of people applying Strait Path real estate to their advantage. These are intended to help you personalize the message and ask yourself what your life will be like when you get on the Strait Path.

APPENDIX C

Recommended Reading

- *The Answer: Grow Any Business, Achieve Financial Freedom, and Live an Extraordinary Life* by John Assaraf and Murray Smith
- *As a Man Thinketh* by James Allen
- *Business as a Calling: Work and the Examined Life* by Michael Novak
- *Cashflow Quadrant: Rich Dad's Guide to Financial Freedom* by Robert T. Kiyosaki
- *The E-Myth Revisited: Why Most Small Businesses Don't Work and What to Do About It* by Michael E. Gerber
- *The Good Earth* by Pearl S. Buck
- *Killing Sacred Cows: Overcoming the Financial Myths That Are Destroying Your Prosperity* by Garrett B. Gunderson

- *Launching a Leadership Revolution* by Chris Brady & Orrin Woodward
- *Let Your Life Speak: Listening for the Voice of Vocation* by Parker J. Palmer
- *Magnificent Obsession* by Lloyd C. Douglas
- *The Master Key to Riches* by Napoleon Hill
- *Positive Imaging: The Powerful Way to Change Your Life* by Norman Vincent Peale
- *The Prosperity Paradigm* by Steve D'Annunzio
- *Rich Dad, Poor Dad: What the Rich Teach Their Kids About Money That the Poor and Middle Class Do Not!* by Robert T. Kiyosaki
- *The Richest Man in Babylon: The Success Secrets of the Ancients* by George S. Clason
- *Think and Grow Rich* by Napoleon Hill
- *Thou Shall Prosper: Ten Commandments for Making Money* by Rabbi Daniel Lapin
- *Atlas Shrugged* by Ayn Rand

Index

15 percent rule
    finding properties using, 96, 98, 104–5, 112, 126
    investment success and, 59
    overview, 2, 37, 39
401(k)s and IRAs, 14–16, 19–23, 31–32, 55, 78–81
1031 exchanges, 179–80

A

abundance mindset, 23, 24–26
accumulated option payments, 155, 157, 158, 163–64, 167
accumulation mindset. *See also* investor mindset
    401(k)s and, 14–16, 19–23, 31–32, 78–81
    failure of, 17–18, 31–32
    home equity pitfalls, 16–18

introduction, 13–14
market volatility, 57–58
paradigm shift from, 13–14
real estate investing *versus*, 20–23, 24–26, 185
risk and, 6–7, 14, 17, 19–23, 53–55
scarcity mindset and, 24–25
"Acres of Diamonds" (Conwell lecture), 78
action (law of now), 29–31
activity *versus* productivity, 52–53
additional option consideration, 155
adjustable rate mortgages (ARMs), 139
applicant qualification, 164–66
applications, 164–66
appraisals, 68, 113, 133–35. *See also* comparative market analysis (CMA)

appraised value, 102–3, 157
appreciation, 61
ARMs (adjustable rate mortgages), 139
Assaraf, John, 53
assets
  creative financing, 41–42, 84
  identification and leverage, 35, 78–83, 87–91, 173–74, 181–82

B
banking industry, 40, 137–39, 141
basements, 115, 116
bathroom comparables, 114–15
bedroom comparables, 114–15
biblical metaphors, 5–6
bonus equity (credited consideration), 154–55, 157, 158, 163–64, 167
Boston College, 19
buyer/seller contract language, 167

C
Carnegie, Dale, 21
Carroll, Lewis, 92–93
cash flow
  goals, 83, 91
  interest rates and, 136
  from lease options, 69
  from livable condition homes, 38
  loan options and, 40–41
  as profit center, 60
  without rental efforts, 7, 47, 73
Clason, George, 174
collaboration, 182–85
comparables, 113–16

comparative market analysis (CMA), 113, 115, 116–25, 135
Compassionate Financing
  applicant qualification, 164–66
  appraisals and, 135, 157
  bonus equity, 154–55, 158, 163–64, 167
  content *versus* context, 189–90
  contracts, 146, 153–55, 166–69
  debt-to-income ratios and, 41, 141–42
  lease options and, 43–44, 69–71, 147, 148–49, 153–55, 156–59
  livable condition homes and, 37–38, 100–104
  marketing, 159–64, 168
  mechanics to meaning, 189–90, 193–95
  money views, 187–89, 199–200
  myths and fallacies, 190–92
  overview, 42–46, 147–52
  profitability, 6–7, 44–45, 58–62, 66–67
  property maintenance, 45, 70, 100–104
  renting comparison with, 66–67, 103, 141–42, 147–48
  service component, 6–7, 42–46, 56, 150, 193–95
  stewardship, 195–201
  sustainability, 50–51, 56, 59, 73, 150, 169, 196
competition for homes, 106
content *versus* context, 189–90

contracts, 125, 146, 153–55, 166–69
Conwell, Russell, 78
corporate structure of investments, 140
creative financing, 41–42, 84
credited consideration (bonus equity), 154–55, 157, 158, 163–64, 167
credit/equity contract language, 153–54, 167
credit scores and reports, 81, 83–85, 130–33, 140, 165–66
critical mass
    collaboration and, 182–85
    discipline and, 36, 92–93, 172–75
    exponential growth and, 175–80
    gratification delay and, 172–75
    infinite growth and, 180–82
    leverage and, 78–83, 87–91, 108, 137–39, 173–74, 181–84
    momentum and, 89–90, 91
    overview, 46–47, 171–72
    repetition, 92, 111–12, 171, 176–77
    speed and, 38–39, 52, 96–97, 107, 111, 112

D

D'Annunzio, Steve, 188, 196
debt-to-income ratios, 41, 131–33, 141–42
delegation, 182–85
discipline, 36, 92–93, 172–75
disclosures, 144
discount equity. *See also* 15 percent rule
    market value and, 59–60, 104–7
    median home price and, 37–38, 65, 96, 97–100, 105, 112, 157
    MLS and, 107–13
    at purchase, 10, 104–8
distress sales, 71–73, 107, 108, 110–11
down payments, 43, 44, 60, 149, 153–54, 163–65, 166

E

Earl, Steve, 28, 177–79
effort element, 6–7, 52–53
Employee Benefit Research Institute, 19
The E-Myth Revisited (Gerber), 184
endurance or discipline, 36, 92–93, 172–75
entitlement mentality, 192
equitable interest, 166
equity. *See also* discount equity
    accumulated option, 155, 157, 158, 163–64, 167
    bonus, 154–55, 158, 163–64, 167
    building, 85–87, 90
    calculating, 104
    in contract language, 167
    pitfalls, 16–18
    at purchase, 10, 104–8
evaluation
    comparables, 114–16
    examples, 118–24
    market value, 104–7, 116–25
    using CMA, 113, 115, 116–25, 135

F

Fair Isaac Corporation (FICO), 130

financial liberation
   content *versus* context, 189–90
   mechanics to meaning, 189, 190, 193–95
   money *versus*, 187–89, 199–200
   myths and fallacies, 190–92
   stewardship and, 195–201
financing
   creative, 41–42, 84
   investor qualification, 83–85, 136
   leverage, 78–83, 87–91, 108, 137–39, 173–74, 181–84
   loans, 40–42, 130–33, 136, 137–39, 140
   mortgage brokers, 40, 97, 137–41
   tenant assistance with, 43–44, 70, 150, 158–59
finding phase
   comparables, 113–16
   equity positions and, 104–8
   livable condition homes, 37–38, 100–104
   market value, 104–7, 116–25
   MLS listings, 37, 106–13, 114
   negotiation, 38, 125–28, 138
   overview, 37–39, 95–97
   price criteria, 37–38, 65, 96, 97–100, 105, 112, 157
   property criteria, 37–38, 99
   realtor aid in, 37, 107–11, 112, 124–25
   speed in, 38–39, 52, 96–97, 107, 111, 112
finished percentage comparables, 116
fix-and-flip homes, 52–53, 64–69, 134–35, 178
fixer-upper homes, 38, 61, 100
flyers, 163–64
Ford, Henry, 183

G

gambling *versus* investing, 17, 23, 53–55
game plan. *See* planning phase
Gates, Bill and Melinda, 193–94
Gerber, Michael, 53, 184
Gladwell, Malcolm, 175–76
goals, investor. *See also* planning phase
   first property purchase, 85–87
   growth calculator, 180
   leverage, 87–89
   momentum, 89–90
   overview, 35–36, 140, 176–77
   traditional financing qualification, 83–85
gratification delay, 172–75
growth
   exponential, 175–80
   infinite, 180–82

H

Hill, Napoleon, 21, 28
home equity pitfalls, 16–18
home inspections, 143–44
homeowners insurance, 145
homes
   appraised value of, 102–3, 157
   comparables relevance, 114–16

fix-and-flip, 52–53, 64–69, 134–35, 178
fixer-uppers, 38, 61, 100
livable condition, 37–38, 100–104
luxury, 98–100
median price, 37–38, 65, 96, 97–100, 105, 112, 157
single-family, 37, 99
home warranties, 144–45

I

income, 81, 131. *See also* debt-to-income ratios
inflation, 16, 17
inspections, 143–44
insurance, 145
interest rates *versus* profitability, 41, 135–37
investments. *See* accumulation mindset; real estate investment elements; real estate investment options; stock market investments
investor mindset
  Law of Now and, 29–31
  possibility attitudes of, 26–29
  success definition, 23–26
IRAs and 401(k)s, 14–16, 19–23, 31–32, 55, 78–81

J

job history, 81, 83–85, 131

L

Launching a Leadership Revolution (Woodward), 29
Law of Now, 29–31
layout (type of home) comparables, 115
lease length, 154
lease options, 43–44, 69–71, 147, 148–49, 153–55, 156–59
lease payments, 154
leverage, 78–83, 87–91, 108, 137–39, 173–74, 181–84
liability protection, 140, 145–46
lifestyle decisions, 173–75, 190, 191
limited-liability corporations (LLCs), 140, 145–46
liquidated damage, 167
listing date comparables, 116
livable condition homes, 37–38, 100–104
loans, 40–42, 130–33, 136, 137–39, 140
location comparables, 116
luxury homes, 98–100

M

maintenance and repairs, 38, 45, 64, 70, 100–104
marketing, 159–64, 168
market value
  appraisals and, 102–3, 113, 133–35, 157
  CMA and, 113
  determining, 116–25

perceived value *versus*, 52–53, 68, 102–7
price per square foot and, 110
purchase price *versus*, 59–60, 154, 156
market volatility, 6–7, 57–58, 97–98, 157
McKelvy, Jack, 102
median home prices, 37–38, 65, 96, 97–100, 105, 112, 157
MLS (Multiple Listing Service), 37, 106–13, 114, 115, 116–25
momentum, 89–90, 91, 92–93
money *versus* financial liberation, 187–89, 199–200
monthly equity (accumulated option), 155, 157, 158, 163–64, 167
monthly payments, 165
mortgage brokers, 40, 97, 137–41
Multiple Listing Service (MLS), 37, 106–13, 114, 115, 116–25
mutual funds, 17, 19
myths and fallacies, 190–92

N
National Board of Realtors, 144
negotiation, 38, 125–28, 138

O
open houses, 162–64
opportunity costs, 203–5
option consideration
    down payment, 43, 44, 60, 149, 153–54, 163–65, 166
    monthly, 155

option purchase agreements, 166–67

P
partnering, 41–42, 81–82, 84–85, 180–82
planning phase
    asset identification and leverage, 35, 78–83, 87–91
    building equity, 90
    discipline, 36, 92–93, 172–75
    momentum, 89–90, 91, 92–93
    overview, 34–36, 77–78
    preparation, 83–85, 90
    purchasing, 85–87, 90
    ten-year goals, 35–36, 83–92, 140, 176–77, 180
possibility attitude, 26–29
power teams, 182–85
prequalification, 136
price
    comparables, 116
    median, 37–38, 65, 96, 97–100, 105, 112, 157
    negotiation, 38, 125–28, 138
    purchase, 154, 157–58
price per square foot test, 110
productivity *versus* activity, 52–53
profitability, 6–7, 41, 44–45, 58–62, 66–67, 135–37
purchase appraisals, 113, 133–35
purchase price, 154, 157–58
purchasing phase
    appraisals, 68, 133–35
    buyer protection tools, 142–46
    debt-to-income ratios, 41, 131–33,

141–42
first property, 85–87
loan options, 137–39
loan qualification, 130–33
loans, 40–42, 130–33, 136, 137–39, 140
mortgage brokers, 40, 97, 137–41
overview, 39–42, 129–30
profits *versus* interest rates, 41, 135–37

Q

qualifying applicants, 164–66

R

Real Estate Firm, 178
Real Estate Investment Companies (REIC), 2, 10–11, 95–96, 158–59, 178, 181, 185
real estate investment elements
    effort, 6–7, 52–53
    introduction, 49–51
    market volatility, 6–7, 57–58, 97–98, 157
    overview, 6–7
    profitability, 6–7, 44–45, 58–62, 66–67
    risk, 6–7, 53–55
    service, 6–7, 42–46, 56, 150, 193–95
    summary, 73
    time, 6–7, 51–52
real estate investment options
    distress sales, 71–73, 107, 108, 110–11

fix-and-flip, 52–53, 64–69, 134–35, 178
fixer-uppers, 38, 61, 100
lease options, 43–44, 69–71, 147, 148–49, 153–55, 156–59
rentals, 61, 63–64, 66–67, 103, 141–42, 147–48
Real Estate Purchase Contracts (REPCs), 125
realtors, 37, 107–11, 112, 124–25
references, applicant, 165
REIC (Real Estate Investment Companies), 2, 10–11, 95–96, 158–59, 178, 181, 185
REIC investor stories, 3–4, 18, 54–55, 74, 155–56
relevance of comparables, 114–16
rentals, 61, 63–64, 66–67, 103, 141–42, 147–48
rent-to-own programs. *See* Compassionate Financing
repairs and maintenance, 38, 45, 64, 70, 100–104
repetition of process, 92, 111–12, 171, 176–77
residential lease agreements, 166
retirement myth, 191
retirement plans, 14–16, 17, 19–23, 31–32, 55, 78–81
The Richest Man in Babylon (Clason), 174
risk, 6–7, 14, 17, 19–23, 53–55

S

sandwich financing, 41, 84

Say, Jean-Baptiste, 78
scarcity mindset, 24–25
seller's disclosures, 144
series LLCs, 140
service to individuals and community, 6–7, 42–46, 56, 150, 193–95
signs, marketing, 159–61
Social Security, 8, 16
"someday" fallacy, 192
Soul Purpose, 188
speed element, 38–39, 52, 96–97, 107, 111, 112
square footage comparables, 114
stewardship, 195–201
stock market investments. *See also* accumulation mindset
    401(k) trap, 14–16, 19–23, 31–32
    market volatility, 57–58
    paradigm shift from, 14, 26, 78–81
    risk and, 14, 17, 19–23, 53–55
Strait Path real estate system. *See also* Compassionate Financing; critical mass; finding phase; planning phase; purchasing phase
    biblical metaphors, 5–6
    core elements, 6–7
    foundations, 7–11
    introduction, 1–6, 33–34
    methodology, 7
Strategic Lending, 138, 139
sustainability, 50–51, 56, 59, 73, 150, 169, 196

T

taxes, 61, 79–80, 179–80
teamwork, 182–85
telephone calls, handling, 161–62
tenant/landlord contract language, 167
tenants
    financing assistance for, 43–44, 70, 150, 158–59
    qualifying, 164–66
time element, 6–7, 51–52
The Tipping Point (Gladwell), 175–76
Tracy, Brian, 197
A Treatise on Political Economy (Say), 78
Trump, Donald, 53

W

walk-through visual inspections, 143
Wall Street Journal, 19
warranties, 144–45
wealth, 24, 56, 80, 189–90, 193–95, 198–99
Woodward, Orrin, 29
work history, 81, 83–85, 131

Y

year built comparables, 115

Praise for Strait Path Real Estate

"My previous experiences in real estate and investing have involved a lot of time and disorganization, and the results have been very poor—losing my money and my extended family's money. My eyes opened wide when I saw that Strait Path real estate looks at the big picture. The Strait Path system has minimized my time, effort, and risk while providing superior returns, independent of market conditions. My wife and I are really excited as we prepare for our future, help our family, and care for others."—Dennis N.

"I've been an entrepreneur since I first got out of college. I always knew that real estate was something I was interested in. As an entrepreneur, I've learned to recognize that there are systems to everything. I was looking for systems in real estate, and the Strait Path system was it. It's a system that the average person with an average income and job can use to build a portfolio."—Scott E.

"I am in finance, and I have many different investment opportunities available to me. Real estate has been around for a long time, but after meeting with Kris I realized that his process is not the normal real estate investment. He is able to turbocharge real estate investing to maximize the rate of return without gambling the money. Kris walked me through his process and spent as much time with me as I needed. When I bought my first home using his method, it worked better than I could have imagined. The biggest problem was that we have too many people wanting houses. My investments with Strait Path real estate have given me a high rate of return, safety, and control. I am so grateful for being introduced to Kris; it has changed my life and the way I invest."—Lance F.

"To hear how the Strait Path system lays out real estate investing in black-and-white really changed my whole way of thinking. I've been extremely disappointed in our 401(k)s and traditional retirement products and strategies. I feel like we've been fed a giant lie, and Kris Krohn really helped pull the veil from our eyes. We have been given the tools, knowledge, and confidence we need to run the system and to do so competently."—Aaron W.

To read more REIC investor experiences, visit www.reicglobal.com.